Sermons by Jonathan Edwards on the Church

VOLUME I

N) I.   April. 1790.

Heb. 12. 22. 23. 24. But ye are come not
nor from and unto the city of the living [?] the
Heavenly Jerusalem ————————

                              32

The apostle had in some of the preceding verses
been earnestly unpersing the [?] Hebrews or [?]
& [?] to avoid the ways of ther 13. v. &c

              Analysis of the most interesting

and the [?] Great argument that the Apostle
makes use of to inforce this [?] counsel
is that they were come to not Sinai as there
fathers were of old but to not [?] the Heavenly Jerusalem &c
signify of this there is [?] at not for to R-
[?], from [?] then there was at not [?]
[?]. There was a great deal to [?]
from from there their fathers for of old [?]
when they came to not Sinai there was manifested the terrible majesty of G: for the not [?]
[?] with fire with lightning & darkness & tem-
pests and the sound of a trumpet and the voice
of words, [?]ing so the this [?] [?], which
voice was so terrible, [?] indeed that they could
bear not be spoken any more to they and
not [?] that not th[?] not [?] & if

Sermons by Jonathan Edwards on the Church

VOLUME I

How Christians Are Come to Mt. Sion

EDITED BY

Kenneth P. Minkema,
R. Craig Woods, and Thomas A. Koontz

WITH AN INTRODUCTION BY

Wilson H. Kimnach

CASCADE *Books* • Eugene, Oregon

SERMONS BY JONATHAN EDWARDS ON THE CHURCH,
VOLUME I
How Christians Are Come to Mt. Sion

Copyright © 2019 Jonathan Edwards Center. All rights reserved. Except for brief quotations in critical publications or reviews, no part of this book may be reproduced in any manner without prior written permission from the publisher. Write: Permissions, Wipf and Stock Publishers, 199 W. 8th Ave., Suite 3, Eugene, OR 97401.

Cascade Books
An Imprint of Wipf and Stock Publishers
199 W. 8th Ave., Suite 3
Eugene, OR 97401

www.wipfandstock.com

PAPERBACK ISBN: 978-1-5326-4909-7
HARDCOVER ISBN: 978-1-5326-4910-3
EBOOK ISBN: 978-1-5326-4911-0

Cataloguing-in-Publication data:

Names: Edwards, Jonathan, 1703–1758, author. | Minkema, Kenneth P., editor. | Woods, R. Craig, editor. | Koontz, Thomas A., editor. | Kimnach, Wilson H., contributor.

Title: Sermons by Jonathan Edwards on the church, volume I : how Christians are come to Mt. Sion / edited by Kenneth P. Minkema, R. Craig Woods, and Thomas A. Koontz, with an introduction by Wilson H. Kimnach.

Description: Eugene, OR : Cascade Books, 2019 | Includes bibliographical references and index.

Identifiers: ISBN 978-1-5326-4909-7 (paperback) | ISBN 978-1-5326-4910-3 (hardcover) | ISBN 978-1-5326-4911-0 (ebook)

Subjects: LCSH: Edwards, Jonathan, 1703–1758. | Bible—Hebrews—Criticism, interpretation, etc. | Bible—Hebrews 12:22–24—Criticism, interpretation, etc. | Preaching—United States—History—18th century. | Sermons. | Pastoral theology.

Classification: LCC BX7233.E42 E25 2019 (print) | LCC BX7233.E42 (ebook)

Manufactured in the U.S.A.

Table of Contents

List of Illustrations	vii
List of Contributors	ix
Preface	xi
Edwards the Preacher	1
by Wilson H. Kimnach	
Historical Context	15
How Christians Are Come to Mt. Sion	35
Index	125

List of Illustrations

The first page of booklet one of the sermon series   ii
on Hebrews 12:22–24 (Courtesy Beinecke Rare Book &
Manuscript Library, Yale University)

List of Contributors

Dr. Wilson H. Kimnach is the Presidential Professor in the Humanities (Emeritus), Bridgeport University, and General Sermon Editor of *The Works of Jonathan Edwards*.

Dr. Kenneth P. Minkema is the Executive Editor and Director of the Jonathan Edwards Center, Yale University, and Research Scholar at Yale Divinity School.

R. Craig Woods retired as Director of Information Technology at Virginia Tech, with degrees in Computer Science, and serves as an elder in the Associate Reformed Presbyterian Church.

Thomas A. Koontz is a practicing architect, with degrees in architecture from Kent State University and Virginia Tech. He is a member of the Jonathan Edwards Center's Global Sermon Editing Project.

Preface

This first volume of *Sermons by Jonathan Edwards on the Church* contains a previously unpublished discourse by Edwards on Hebrews 12:22–24, preached in early 1740, on the very cusp of the transatlantic religious movement that would become known as "The Great Awakening," the New England phase of which began later that year. To assist the reader, preceding the series are two introductions that describe Edwards' preaching style and method and provide an historical context for the series itself.

A Note on Edwards' Text
Edwards' sermon series *How Christians Are Come to Mt. Sion* is printed here in full for the first time from the original manuscripts as transcribed and edited by the staff of the Jonathan Edwards Center at Yale University, with the assistance of volunteer editors. These volunteers were recruited through the Jonathan Edwards Center's online community-sourcing initiative, The Global Sermon Editing Project. Begun in 2012, this innovative program presented the opportunity for non-specialists to be trained to edit Edwards' sermons from proofread transcripts. It attracted hundreds of volunteers from over a dozen countries. The passion and perseverance of these individuals is manifest in the book you are viewing now, and in ones to come. Heartfelt gratitude and respect go out to all who participated, and particularly the colleagues who contributed directly to this volume.

In presenting these texts, the editors have followed the conventions of the Yale Edition of *The Works of Jonathan Edwards* (twenty-six volumes, 1957–2008), regularizing spelling, capitalization, and format. Preserved here are Edwards' own words, punctuated in an eighteenth-century style. Because the manuscript was largely uncorrected by Edwards—it was, after all, for his personal use for public delivery—there are inconsistencies in number, style, and tense, which, as a rule, are left as they are; any changes are footnoted. In any given manuscript there are a great number of deletions, so here only deletions of significant textual importance are footnoted. Readers may find Edwards' manner of writing challenging at first, but we believe the effort to understand Edwards in his own terms, in his own idiom, and to get a sense of the immediacy of his preaching, will be rewarded. Finally, Scripture quotes are rendered according to the King James Bible, which was the version Edwards used.

Readers will note that throughout this discourse Edwards uses both "Mt Sion" and "Mt Zion" interchangeably. In the King James Bible, Mt. Sion is identified with Mt. Hermon, a physical location in northern Palestine, but it is also called "the city of the living God" in Hebrews 12, the text of the discourse presented here. Likewise, Mt. Zion is usually the appellation for David's city, Jerusalem, but it, too, is used to identify the heavenly city. Biblical commentators in Edwards' day associated Sion with Sinai, and so saw Sion and Zion as figures of the old and new covenants. So did Edwards. He goes back and forth in spellings, apparently indiscriminately, but we have retained his spelling in the event that there is an as-yet-undetectable pattern.

One feature of the text presented below bears special explanation: cases of editorial interpolation. These are of two types. First, outright omissions by Edwards, and lacunae in the manuscript, are filled by insertions in square brackets ([,]). Secondly, one aspect of the outlinish nature of this sermon series is easily seen in the many dashes of varying lengths that Edwards drew at the beginning, in the middle, and at the end of statements. These dashes represent repeated words or phrases, as well as connective pieces of sentences, that Edwards would have provided extemporaneously. Where these dashes have been editorially amplified, they are surrounded by curly brackets ({,}).

PREFACE

The manuscripts are in the Edwards Collection, Beinecke Rare Book and Manuscript Library, Yale University. Transcripts may be viewed on the Jonathan Edwards Center's website, edwards.yale.edu. The first half of the introduction below, by Wilson H. Kimnach, is adapted from his larger discussion of "Jonathan Edwards' Art of Prophesying" in *The Works of Jonathan Edwards*, 10, *Sermons and Discourses*, 1720–1723 (New Haven, Yale University Press, 1990), 21–27, 36–42.

Readers of this volume may also be interested in consulting previous publications in this series by Cascade Books, printed in 2012:

Jonathan Edwards on the Matthean Parables, edited by Kenneth P. Minkema and Adriaan C. Neele:
> Volume I: *The Parable of the Wise and Foolish Virgins*
> Volume II: *The Parable of the Sower and the Seed*
> Volume III: *The Parable of the Net*

Edwards the Preacher

Wilson H. Kimnach

Edwards' Thoughts on Preaching

Jonathan Edwards was in full agreement with his teachers respecting the exalted status of the preacher. For though his writings occasionally contain references to "earthen vessels" and sometimes emphasize the preacher's humble situation as a son of Adam, it is much more common for Edwards to see the preacher as a man exalted and even transfigured by his calling. Indeed, in some of the earliest entries in his "Miscellanies," nos. mm, qq, and 40, Edwards attempts to define to his own satisfaction the nature of the call, the limits and quality of a minister's influence in society, and the power in preaching or teaching the divine Word.

> Yet it is clear that those that are in the New Testament called ministers are not every private Christian, and consequently if [any] such remain now as are there spoken of, they are distinct from other Christians. 'Tis clear they are born undistinguished; from this 'tis clear they are distinguished afterwards. 'Tis also evident that they are distinguished some way or other by Christ....[1]

---

1. "Miscellanies" no. *mm*, in *Works of Jonathan Edwards*, 13, "Miscellanies," *a*-500, edited by Thomas A. Schafer (New Haven: Yale University Press, 1994), 187. After initial citation, volumes in *The Works of Jonathan Edwards* (New Haven: Yale University Press, 1957–2008) will be referred to as "WJE" plus volume and page numbers. Texts by JE published in the Jonathan Edwards Center's website (edwards.yale.edu) will be referred to as "WJEO" plus the volume number.

This earliest entry on the office of the preacher calls attention to the essentially aristocratic bias of Edwards, which is quite in keeping with his upbringing, while it also demonstrates his characteristic propensity to rethink every important aspect of his life "from the ground up," regardless of his background and training. He may not seriously question the assumptions of his heritage, but he will insist upon a personal formulation of that heritage in his own written words.

The preacher is, then, a "chosen one" with a distinct charisma as a result of his call to serve Christ. He is invested with a capacity and right to instruct, lead, and judge his people;[2] he has no pretension to civil authority, but in the all-important moral and spiritual realms he is, of all human beings, supremely authoritative. "Miscellanies" no. 40 contains early speculations upon the powers that would inhere in the effective preaching of the Word, specifically:

> Without doubt, ministers are to teach men what Christ would have them to do, and to teach them who doth these things and who doth them not; that is, who are Christians and who are not....
>
> Thus, if I in a right manner am become the teacher of a people, so far as they ought to hear what I teach them, so much power I have. Thus, if they are obliged to hear me only because they themselves have chosen me to guide them, and therein declared that they thought me sufficiently instructed in the mind of Christ to teach them, and because I have the other requisites of being their teacher, then I have power as other ministers have in these days. But if it was plain to them that I was under the infallible guidance of Christ, then I should have more power. And if it was plain to all the world of Christians that I was under the infallible guidance of Christ, and [that] I was sent forth to teach the world the will of Christ, then I should have power in all the world. I should have power to teach them what they ought to do, and they would be obliged to hear me; I should have

---

2. WJE 13:188.

power to teach them who were Christians and who not, and in this likewise they would be obliged to hear me.³

As in a daydream, the student-preacher toys with the mystery of the call, and at least by implication ponders the limits and possibilities of the role of a preacher. Could he command the people, or even the world, as a divine messenger? Obviously, there must be some immediate sign, some quality of utterance, that would in itself attest to the supernatural ordination. In this early passage Edwards is already pondering aspects of sermonic style, but characteristically he begins on the most general and profound, most philosophical level. Puritan ministers had always been urged to "preach powerfully," but in this meditation there are new undertones, and "power" clearly relates to a divine investiture that transcends conventional sectarian sanctions. Certainly it seems that Edwards was as well fitted to study the art of preaching under the imperious Solomon Stoddard, his grandfather and predecessor as the pastor of Northampton, Massachusetts, as any man.

Edwards did not pretend to eloquence or a fine style. Indeed, from the first he seems to have made a point of proclaiming his lack of a fine style.

> [T]he practical discourses that follow . . . now appear in that very plain and unpolished dress in which they were first prepared and delivered; which was mostly at a time when the circumstances of the auditory they were preached to, were enough to make a minister neglect, forget, and despise such ornaments as politeness and modishness of style and method, when coming as a messenger from God to souls deeply impressed with a sense of their danger of God's everlasting wrath, to treat with them about their eternal salvation. However unable I am to preach or write politely, if I would, yet I have this to comfort me under such a defect; that God has showed us that he don't need such talents in men to carry on his own work, and that he has been pleased to smile upon and bless a very plain, unfashionable way of preaching. And have we not reason to think that it ever has been,

3. WJE 13:222.

and ever will be, God's manner to bless the foolishness of preaching to save them that believe, let the elegance of language, and excellency of style, be carried to never so great a height, by the learning and wit of the present and future ages?

This passage, from the Preface to *Discourses on Various Important Subjects* (1738),[4] is characteristic of the tone of most of Edwards' prefaces, though the discussion is a little more explicit and fully developed. It is defensive, condemning wit and style out of hand as irrelevant to effective preaching, while also suggesting an incapacity for stylistic excellence on his own part.

Part of this may be explained by Edwards' cultural background that would have taught him to think of rhetoric or eloquence as a thing separable from the logical structure of an argument.[5] Since he was consciously developing a heart-piercing manner of writing that would be as spare and efficient as an arrow, he assumed

---

4. P. v; *The Works of Jonathan Edwards*, 19, *Sermons and Discourses, 1734–1738*, edited by M. X. Lesser (New Haven: Yale University Press, 2001), 797.

5. The peculiar attitude that assumes substance and expression to be distinct and separable was quite widespread in the seventeenth century and occasioned the birth of the "plain style" among preachers and "mathematical plainness" in the Royal Society. While a detailed survey of this significant aspect of JE's cultural background is beyond the scope of this introduction, it should be stated that the crucial factor in that background seems to have been the philosophy of Peter Ramus. With the aid of his colleague, Omer Talon, Ramus devised a new formulation of the relationship between logic and rhetoric, involving the transfer of the classical (Ciceronian) invention, disposition, and memory from the province of rhetoric to that of dialectic. This left only style, apprehended as a matter of figures and tropes, and delivery to rhetoric; rhetoric became the sideshow to thought, a crowd-pleasing (or even crowd-deluding) device. Thus, those who were intent upon the intellectual substance of their expression or were intensely earnest, such as Puritan preachers and the new scientists, tended to condemn and avoid "style" as something adventitious and frivolous. Moreover, those who cultivated rhetoric during the seventeenth century actually did tend to artificiality and ornateness, as might be expected when figures and tropes are seen more or less as ends in themselves. For a detailed discussion of the history behind JE's attitude, and an investigation of the long groping toward what we should today call an organic style, see Wilbur S. Howell's *Logic and Rhetoric in England, 1500–1700* (Princeton: Princeton University Press, 1956).

that "style," being an adventitious decoration, would have to be left out. It would not have struck Edwards that that efficacious verbal expression for which he constantly strove and "style" might be the same thing. Thus he really could spend much of his lifetime studying the theory and practice of language and metaphor without "paying any attention to style." Of course, part of the problem is also that, as in the seventeenth century, preaching styles were associated with theological positions. In Edwards' day many of the most eloquent preachers of the East were suspect in Edwards' eyes of being rationalist, Arminian, or just theologically jejune. He would therefore rather deny excellence in his carefully wrought sermons than be thought—perhaps even by himself—to be a creature of wit and style. He was too serious, too full of thought, and too honest for *style*.

Indeed, if Edwards claimed brilliance of any kind it was the more essential and "substantial" excellence of thought, and once again he saw himself as being out of tune with the times:

> Our discovering the absurdity of the impertinent and abstruse distinctions of the School Divines, may justly give us a distaste of such distinctions as have a show of learning in obscure words, but convey no light to the mind; but I can see no reason why we should also discard those that are clear and rational, and can be made out to have their foundation in truth.

In the same Preface,[6] in a sustained argument of two pages, he defends the virtue of "real" fine distinctions in elaborating the "mysteries" of religion. If, as Cotton Mather contended in *Manuductio ad Ministerium* (1726), his instruction manual for aspiring ministers, reason is natural to the soul of man, then Edwards would have him test this capacity, as he would fully exercise the heart, in the quest of a valid apprehension of divine truths.

Edwards may have been inspired by the example of his father Timothy Edwards, minister of East Windsor, Connecticut, to use the utmost rigor in making convicting arguments, and Stoddard

---

6. P. iii; WJE 19:795-96.

undoubtedly provided the pattern for a potent, "psychological" rhetoric for which Edwards had no name. But having a finer mind and more imagination than either Stoddard or Timothy Edwards, Edwards outperformed each at his specialty while combining elements of both their strategies. His intense interest in the mysterious power of language, however, was apparently innate.

Edwards' matured vision of the ideal preacher is most completely delineated in his ordination sermon on John 5:35, entitled *The True Excellency of a Minister of the Gospel* (1744).[7] There, he insists that a minister must be "both a burning and a shining light"; that "his heart burn with love to Christ, and fervent desires of the advancement of his kingdom and glory," and that "his instructions [be] clear and plain, accommodated to the capacity of his hearers, and tending to convey light to their understandings." This peculiar combination of head and heart, he insists, is absolutely necessary to the success of a preacher:

> When light and heat are thus united in a minister of the gospel, it shows that each is genuine, and of a right kind, and that both are divine. Divine light is attended with heat; and so, on the other hand, a truly divine and holy heat and ardor is ever accompanied with light.

That both heat and light may be acquired by the aspiring preacher, Edwards urges him to be "diligent in [his] studies," "very conversant with the holy Scriptures," and "much in seeking God, and conversing with him by prayer, who is the fountain of light and love." All in all, Edwards' ideal does not seem to be very different from that of the traditional preacher of the time, except that in the full context of the sermon and through the extensive use of light imagery, he suggests a standard of transcendent dedication and nearly mystical fervor that is rare in any age. And like Stoddard before him, Edwards cultivated a subtle personal tone in his rhetoric that, more than any stated principle, demonstrates the risk-taking commitment demanded of the good preacher.

---

7. *The Works of Jonathan Edwards*, 25, *Sermons and Discourses,* 1743–1758, edited by Wilson H. Kimnach (New Haven: Yale University Press, 2006), 82–102.

Edwards is best known for his defenses of passionate emotion, including "hellfire," in revival preaching. And, indeed, in *Religious Affections* he argues that "such means are to be desired, as have much of a tendency to move the affections."[8] Moreover, in *Some Thoughts on the Revival of Religion in New England*, he emphatically insists that

> Though . . . clearness of distinction and illustration, and strength of reason, and a good method, in the doctrinal handling of the truths of religion, is many ways needful and profitable, and not to be neglected . . . [o]ur people don't so much need to have their heads stored, as to have their hearts touched; and they stand in the greatest need of that sort of preaching that has the greatest tendency to do this.[9]

As for "hellfire" preaching in particular, Edwards argues:

> Some talk of it as an unreasonable thing to think to fright persons to heaven; but I think it is a reasonable thing to endeavor to fright persons away from hell . . . 'tis a reasonable thing to fright a person out of an house on fire.

As for the style or manner of "hellfire" preaching, he makes this observation:

> When ministers preach of hell, and warn sinners to avoid it, in a cold manner, though they may say in words that it is infinitely terrible; yet (if we look on language as a communication of our minds to others) they contradict themselves; for actions, as I observed before, have a language to convey our minds, as well as words; and at the same time that such a preacher's words represents the sinner's state as infinitely dreadful, his behavior and manner of speaking contradict it, and show that the preacher don't think so; so that he defeats his own purpose; for

---

8. *The Works of Jonathan Edwards*, 2, *Religious Affections*, edited by John E. Smith (New Haven: Yale University Press, 1959), 121.

9. *The Works of Jonathan Edwards*, 4, *Great Awakening*, edited by C. C. Goen (New Haven: Yale University Press, 1972), 387-88.

the language of his actions, in such a case, is much more effectual than the bare signification of his words.[10]

Edwards might well have extended this comment to include the "gesture of language"—specifically, images and metaphors employed in making an argument concrete—in the case of printed sermons.

In summary, it should be observed that, while Edwards placed no limits on the intensity of emotion that a preacher might attempt to evoke through his preaching, he insisted upon a constant balance and aesthetically pleasing harmony between emotion and thought. Indeed, he insisted that without a duly precise and comprehensive body of theological concepts in the sermon, there is no religion at all.[11]

Edwards' ideal preacher is, then, a figure of commanding intellectual rigor and overwhelming rhetorical power; he strikes a blow for religion simultaneously in the heads and hearts of his auditors, though with an emphasis upon the heart. In the performance of his duty, he shows that he is the peculiarly designated servant of his Master:

> They should imitate [Christ] in the manner of his preaching; who taught not as the Scribes, but with authority, boldly, zealously and fervently; insisting chiefly on the most important things in religion, being much in warning men of the danger of damnation, setting forth the greatness of the future misery of the ungodly; insisting not only on the outward, but also the inward and spiritual duties of religion: being much in declaring the great provocation and danger of spiritual pride, and a self-righteous disposition; yet much insisting on the necessity and importance of inherent holiness, and the practice of piety, . . . wonderfully adapting his discourse to persons, seasons and occasions.[12]

10. WJE 4:247–48.

11. For an extended discussion of JE's ideas on the necessity of intellectual substance in sermons, see his sermon, *The Importance and Advantage of a Thorough Knowledge of Divine Truth*, in WJE 22:80–102.

12. *Christ the Example of Ministers*, WJE 25:339.

If a congregation could "hear and stand it out" under such preaching, there would probably be little hope for the English language as an instrument of salvation.

The Sermon in Edwards' Hands

The development and ultimate deterioration of the sermon form in Edwards' hands will be discussed shortly, but now an attempt must be made to define the formal limits of the Edwardsean sermon at the zenith of its development during the late 1720s, the 1730s, and the very early 1740s (and whenever Edwards had an important preaching occasion in subsequent years and returned to that form and style).[13] This sermon is a formal literary unit consisting of three main divisions, Text, Doctrine, and Application. There is only one significant variation in the form which is called a "lecture." The lecture is differentiated from the sermon only through the altered proportions in the Doctrine and Application. For whereas in the sermon the Application is usually a little longer than the Doctrine and often several times as long, in the lecture the Doctrine is substantially longer than the Application. Perhaps the best-known instance of the lecture variant is *A Divine and Supernatural Light* (1734), which has a doctrine of twenty-three pages, and an Application of a little over three pages in the first edition.

Otherwise, so far as *form* is concerned, a sermon is a sermon—whether pastoral, imprecatory, occasional, doctrinal, or whatever.[14] Of course, this does not mean that the form was ever so fixed as to restrict variations; indeed, there were always so many variations that the very identity of the sermon as a literary form

---

13. The recovery in the early 1980s of JE's original MS of the *Farewell Sermon* (1750) provided confirmation that, though he employed scrap paper in all late sermons, JE returned to writing out all sermons he considered important.

14. Sermons based upon Old Testament texts tend to have longer Doctrines than those based upon New Testament texts, resulting in some lessening of emphasis upon Application in Old Testament-text sermons. This phenomenon seems to result from a necessity for relating Old Testament materials to the gospel message, which is effected in the Doctrine.

seems at times threatened. If the variations possible within the three main divisions are considered, however, it is evident that Edwards never lost sight of the paradigm.

Text

The Text begins the sermon, invariably with the Scripture passage upon which the formal structure of the sermon rests. Indeed, it is the verse citation of the initial Scripture passage, rather than a word or phrase from the Doctrine, that identifies a sermon when it is referred to in Edwards' notebooks. There is no exordium or introduction before the reading of the Scripture text, and there need not be any explication or exegesis after it, if the meaning is obvious, in order to have a complete Text. In the vast majority of sermons, however, there is a brief passage (a page, more or less) of comment and explication following the scriptural passage which Edwards designates the Opening of the Text. The Opening consists of several brief, numbered heads, frequently designated "Observation" or "Inference," in which Edwards defines difficult terms, cites other Scripture passages that parallel or complement the textual passage, and generally explains its meaning. In explication, he is never pedantic, even on those rare occasions when he introduces Hebrew or Greek words to clarify definitions; he explains carefully, but does not belabor small points. Indeed, some students of Edwards have felt the Opening of the Text to be the finest part of the sermon because of Edwards' remarkable ability to narrate the statements and events of the text as immediate experience, and in his narrations he not infrequently displays the talent of a first-rate journalist or novelist. But his narrations present concise sketches rather than murals, and the Text is never long.

Doctrine

Following the Text is the Doctrine, a major portion of most sermons and, structurally, often the most complex. The Doctrine usually begins with a single statement of doctrine, carefully labeled "Doc[trine]." In his inclination to formulate the entire doctrinal message of the sermon in a single statement of doctrine, Edwards was, it seems, a little unusual for his day. Most contemporary preachers tended to formulate two or more equally important statements and list them in parallel at the head of the Doctrine. Although it is Edwards' custom to draw two, three, or four Propositions or Observations from the doctrine immediately after its statement, thus dividing it for "clearing" or full discussion in the body of the Doctrine, the single statement of doctrine brings the entire sermon into a sharp thematic focus, like light rays passing through a lens, if only for a vivid moment.

But there need be no formal statement of doctrine at all. Sometimes, when the Scripture text is a clear, concise statement of thesis in itself and in need of no explication, Text and Doctrine elide and the Scripture quotation becomes the statement of doctrine, or, as Edwards puts it, the doctrine is "supplied." At other times, though rarely in Edwards' best days of preaching, there is no statement labeled "Doc[trine]," but only one or two propositions.[15] In such cases, the Proposition differs not at all from the usual statement of doctrine, unless it be a little less assertive in tone.

After the statement of doctrine and the division of the statement into Propositions, Edwards takes up the propositions, explaining the import of each and developing its implications through Inquiries, Observations, Arguments, and plain numbered heads. Each proposition is also "proved" through Reasons. The term "reason" is actually a generic term for all "proofs" under the Doctrine, and Edwards does not frequently use it as the name for a particular head. The proofs of the doctrine are of two basic types: citations of Scripture (often attended with interpretation), and appeals to human reason and commonplace experience.

---

15. A hallmark of the Stockbridge Indian sermons is that, whether written out or in bare outline, they have nothing labeled "Doc[trine]," but only Propositions or Observations, despite being virtual synopses of earlier sermons which had formal statements of doctrine.

Most of the time, particularly in the shorter and middle-length sermons, the Doctrine ends with the giving of various reasons or proofs. However, each Proposition may have its own Use, Improvement, or Application, especially in the longer sermons. This occurs most often when the various propositions have quite different practical implications, and Edwards feels compelled to spell out the different duties implied by each proposition. However, these uses are within the division of the Doctrine and are not to be confused with the third main division of the sermon. In sermons where such "doctrinal uses" are employed, Edwards often differentiates them from the third main division by calling it the "Application of the Whole."

Application

The Application (or Improvement or Use) is the largest of the three main divisions of the sermon (except in the lecture variant), and in long sermons it may be several times as long as the Text and Doctrine together. It is usually marked by a significant alteration in tone and rhetoric, and by a comparatively simple structure; for whereas the Text and Doctrine are concerned with theory, principle, and precept, the Application is concerned with experience and practice. The Application is directed to specific thoughts, attitudes, and actions of living human beings, and it gives specific advice on these attitudes and actions, in poignant language, in the light of the sermon's doctrine. But as employed by Edwards, the Application also has a subtler use as is indicated by his own statement in this transitional passage between the Doctrine and Application of Genesis 19:14.

> The Improvement we shall make of this doctrine shall be to offer some considerations to make future punishment seem real to you.

In effect, then, the Application is a period of hypothetical experience for Edwards' auditory, a time of living imaginatively, through a "willing suspension of disbelief," a series of fictive experiences created and controlled by the preacher.

Uses

The Application or Improvement is generally structured by division into several Uses. Most of the time, the term "use" is restricted to serving as the categorical name for main heads under the division of "Application" or "Improvement," paralleling "reasons" in the Doctrine. (The two division names, incidentally, are used interchangeably, though "Application" appears to be the favored term after the first few years of preaching.) Thus, there is frequently a Use of Self-examination, or a Use of Consolation, and up to four or five such "specialized" uses, though the concluding use is most often the Use of Exhortation. Each Use is subdivided by Inquiries, Considerations, and plain numbered heads, and a list of Considerations or Directions generally concludes the Use of Exhortation.

There are several "paired" heads, such as Objection-Consideration, Enquiry-Answer, and Positive-Negative, that may appear under any one of the three major divisions of the sermon as they are needed, as may such heads as Inference, Observation, or Inquiry. In fact, it should be noted that the minor heads are generally employed in a very flexible way, and are inserted wherever they fit. Few are used only in the Text, Doctrine, or the Application.

In order to have a complete Edwardsean sermon, then, there must be an identifying passage of Scripture at the beginning and an Application (of the whole) at the end; in the middle, there must be a doctrinal discussion of the Bible text, though not necessarily an Opening of the Text or an explicitly labeled "Doc[trine]." The minimal requirements are comparatively easy to describe; the difficulties arise when one attempts to define the "outer limits" of the sermon form.

First, there is the problem of literary form versus pulpit performance. Edwards sometimes speaks of a single preaching session in the pulpit, and that portion of a long sermon which might be preached in one session, as a sermon; but he also speaks of a complex literary unit, which includes several clearly marked preaching units within it, as a sermon. Apparently he was not alone in his ambiguity, for in several eighteenth-century editions his longer sermons are printed as a series of sermons (according to preaching units) rather than as the single long sermons that, according to the form, they are. Such printing conventions preserve the root sense of the Latin *sermo*, which means "talk"; moreover, they preserve the spirit of the seventeenth-century New England sermon as a speech act only incidentally preserved in print. When editing his own sermons for the press, however, Edwards scrupulously called sermons of more than one preaching unit "discourses," as in *Discourses on Various Important Subjects*, where some pieces are of one preaching unit and others of more. Modern readers especially must treat the Text-Doctrine-Application unit—however long—as a literary unit: otherwise, they will probably miss theme, logic, and form altogether.

Even when one admits that a sermon may be of any length, as long as it is carefully constructed, without losing its formal unity, there is the complication created by the "paired sermons" and the sermon series. In the case of the paired sermons, Edwards may write two sermons on the same text to be preached in series; however, they share nothing, not even the Opening of the Text, beyond the initial Scripture text. Obviously they are two sermons, though they may, if they are brief, be delivered on the same day. Then there is the variant in which Edwards announces two doctrines in two sermons, but develops only the first doctrine in the first sermon and only the second doctrine in the second sermon. Again, though the sermons are obviously meant to go together, they are formally separated. Such variations, when multiplied, led to the several sermon series that Edwards wrote and preached in the 1730s, including the one presented here.

Obviously, somewhere between the morning-and-afternoon sermon, divided between the Doctrine and the Application so that it could fill the entire Sabbath-day services, and the over-two-hundred-page, thirty-preaching-unit sermon series, the form of the sermon begins to disintegrate. Edwards became a master of his inherited sermon form, but in the 1730s, at the zenith of his mastery, he began experimenting artistically with the sermon. He apparently did everything he could do without actually abandoning the old form entirely, and the only possible conclusion one can draw from the manuscript evidence of his experiments is that he was searching, consciously or unconsciously, for a formal alternative to the sermon itself.

Introduction: Historical Context

In April 1740, Jonathan Edwards, minister of Northampton, Massachusetts, preached a discourse on Hebrews 12:22–24 comprising eight sermons. At this point, he had been the senior pastor of that town for just over a decade, and had seen his congregation through the historic Connecticut Valley Awakening of the mid-1730s, when several hundred souls were reportedly savingly converted, ushering in a new period of religious fervor known collectively as "The Great Awakening" beginning in 1740.

Edwards' practice over the several years previous to his performance on Hebrews 12 had been to deliver lengthy, complex discourses, as seen in the series on Matthew 25 (*True and False Christians*), preached from November 1737 to February 1738; on 1 Corinthians 13 (posthumously published as *Charity and Its Fruits*), from April to October 1738; and on Isaiah 51:8 (also posthumously published as *A History of the Work of Redemption*), from March to August 1739.[16] While he may be remembered for

---

16. For the printed versions of these discourses, see *Sermons by Jonathan Edwards on the Matthean Parables, Volume I: True and False Christians (On the Parable of the Wise and Foolish Virgins)*, edited by Kenneth P. Minkema, Adriaan C. Neele and Bryan McCarthy (Eugene, OR: Cascade, 2012); *Charity and Its Fruits* in *The Works of Jonathan Edwards, Volume 8, Ethical* Writings, edited by Paul Ramsey (New Haven: Yale University Press, 1989), 123–98; and *The Works of Jonathan Edwards, Volume 9, A History of the Work of Redemption*, edited by John F. Wilson, Jr. (New Haven: Yale University Press, 1989). Note that the latter volume prints the text of the original sermon series, while that printed in Edinburgh in 1774 was revised by Jonathan Edwards Jr. and John Erskine.

Sermons on the Church by Jonathan Edwards

shorter sermons, earlier and later, such as *A Divine and Supernatural Light* (1734) and *Sinners in the Hands of an Angry God* (1741), this interim period between revivals actually can be identified as Edwards' most mature and accomplished as a homiletician, when he was giving his most sustained attention to his craft by virtue of extended exegesis of biblical texts and of comprehensive application to his congregants' experiences. Through these monumental efforts, Edwards secured his place in the distinguished pantheon of Reformed preachers.

The Connecticut Valley Awakening, which had run from late 1734 until the spring of 1735, was by the spring of 1740 a memory, a benchmark, memorialized in Edwards' famous *Faithful Narrative of a Surprising Work of God* (1737), which described the nature and unfolding of revival in detail for others to emulate; and in *Discourses on Various Important Subjects* (1738), which gathered five important sermons from the period. As a result of these, Northampton and Edwards had achieved international fame within and outside of the pan-Protestant international evangelical network. Since then, however, the spiritual state of the town had been flat, "dead" and "dull," as Edwards described it. Instead, as if literally building on their notoriety, the town turned to architecture: constructing a new meetinghouse, dedicated on Christmas Day 1737, and a new town house. The news of war between England and Spain in October 1739 only further turned people's attention to more temporal matters.

Edwards, meanwhile, strove to coax back the revival spirit, comparing his flock's decidedly unchristian behavior with what it had been during the glory days of '35. "Viciousness," contention, hard business practices, "backbiting," and the like were the order of the day. But there was change in the air; the gyre of providence was turning. In November 1739, Edwards received a letter from George Whitefield, then in New York City, in the midst of his first preaching tour of America. Although unable at present because of his busy schedule, Whitefield hoped to come to Northampton in a few months.[17] Edwards replied with a hearty invitation in Feb-

---

17. George Whitefield to Edwards, Nov. 16, 1739, in *Works of George*

ruary 1740, though also with a warning that the hearts of New Englanders, who had so long enjoyed great preaching, were hardened more than others. So Edwards and his fellow clergy awaited the arrival of Whitefield later in the year. But for now, Edwards contented himself with learning what he could, via newspapers, letters, and word of mouth, of the stirrings of the Spirit in England and Wales, especially through the preaching of the Wesleys and Howell Harris.

Expectation was interrupted by the arrival in February 1740 of another guest, a most unwelcome one: measles. News of its spread caused Edwards to cancel a journey to Hadley, downriver, to attend a fast, citing his own weak condition and the advanced pregnancy of his wife Sarah Pierpont Edwards (who would give birth to Susannah on June 20).[18] The disease spread through the region, laying low thousands and killing hundreds. Several of Edwards' children came down with it, but they were spared from the mortality that so many other families experienced.

By April, and the arrival of spring following a snowstorm in mid-March, the epidemic was abating, and Edwards was again on the road between the sabbaths on which he delivered most, if not all, of his latest sermonic effort. He attended the meeting of the Hampshire County Association of Ministers on April 8, which met in West Springfield at the home of his sister Esther and her husband Samuel Hopkins. Six days later he was in Westfield to preach at the funeral of minister Nehemiah Bull.[19]

The series sermons on Hebrews 12, with its exploration of the ascent of the church to Mt. Zion, is not without precedents or foreshadowings in Edwards' preaching and other writings. For example, in the contemporaneously written entry on vv. 22–24 in the

---

Whitefield (1771), 1:121–22. On Whitefield's visit to Northampton, see George M. Marsden, *Jonathan Edwards: A Life* (New Haven: Yale University Press, 2003), 201–12.

18. Edwards to Rev. Isaac Chauncy, Feb. 18, 1740, in *The Works of Jonathan Edwards, Volume 16, Letters and Personal* Writings, edited by George S. Claghorn (New Haven: Yale University Press 1998), 82.

19. See Edwards, MS sermon on Matt. 14:12(a), no. 543, April 4, 1740 (Beinecke Rare Book and Manuscript Library, Yale University).

"Blank Bible," Edwards quotes English Nonconformist educator Philip Doddridge's *Family Expositor* (6 vols., 1739–48) on a theme that he explores in his own treatment: the "milder" manifestation of God on Mt. Zion than on Mt. Sinai when the Ten Commandments were given. In a note on v. 23, he quotes Puritan theologian and Oxford don John Owen's *Excercitations on the Epistle to the Hebrews* (3 vols., 1680–88) on the nature of the "first born" and on "the spirits of just men made perfect."[20] As was his practice elsewhere, Edwards reached out to respected expositors to confirm and compare with his own readings.

His sermons from early 1740 also contain some anticipation of the theme of the "ascent" or glorification of saints and the church as a whole. Indeed, the church militant and glorified was the focus of his attention in his discourse on Hebrews.[21] From January, a sermon on the Parable of the Prodigal Son, in which the prodigal, like all saints, is clothed with gorgeous robes in preparation for the heavenly feast, harks to the larger treatment of the church coming to Zion; as does the sermon on Heb. 9:15–16, considering the covenant of grace as Christ's "last will and testament," by which the church is given heaven, and where "God the Judge," who will figure prominently in the Hebrews series, appears. And in the sermon on Philip. 3:17, delivered the following month, the Apostle Paul is presented as the "complete Christian," the culmination of whose journey is the heavenly Zion.[22] Thus the discourse operates both in the present and in the future: Christians come to Mt. Zion in their conversion on earth, but they are also still arriving, continuously and collectively, and will finally arrive after the day of judgment.

20. "Blank Bible" entries on Heb. 12:22–24 and on v. 23, in *The Works of Jonathan Edwards, Volume 24, The "Blank Bible,"* edited by Stephen J. Stein (New Haven: Yale University Press, 2006), 1162–63.

21. See Rhys Bezzant, *Jonathan Edwards and the Church* (New York: Oxford University Press, 2014); and Michael J. McClymond & Gerald R. McDermott, *The Theology of Jonathan Edwards* (New York: Oxford University Press, 2012), 251–64.

22. For sermons that come after but repeat themes, see no. 552, Rom. 11:7, on elect "obtaining"; and no. 555, Luke 10:42, which considers the combination of "good things" saints will enjoy in heaven (WJEO, Vol. 55).

As even this brief survey of Edwards' sermons from early in 1740 reveals, they did not spring up in isolation; they were part of an intricate web of evolving personal and public concerns and interests. Therefore it is helpful, and important, to note certain other continuities between the discourse on Hebrews 12 and themes that Edwards was considering elsewhere, particularly in his "Miscellanies," his series of theological and philosophical notebooks.

One issue that Hebrews 12 brought up for Edwards was that of the "separate state" of departed souls. Rather than saying that the souls of the deceased go to a state of limbo where they "sleep" until the day of judgment, Edwards, in conversation with contemporary figures such as English theologian and hymnwriter Isaac Watts, argued strongly and consistently that the souls of both the damned and the elect go to hades or heaven, there to await the final sentence. In the period before his sermon series on Hebrews 12, Edwards explored this teaching in "Miscellanies" nos. 60, 666, and 710.[23] Interestingly, the question of separate states most often came up in considerations of hades and of damned souls, but this usually led Edwards to the status of elect souls. For Edwards, the day of judgment would not be an anticlimactic event, because, as he writes in later "Miscellanies" such as nos. 952, 1121, and 1126, both hell and heaven would be changed afterwards: hell becoming intensely more miserable, and heaven intensely more glorious.[24]

In *Charity and Its Fruits*, especially in its concluding sermon, Edwards had also described the nature of heaven. One aspect of the "upper world" on which he focused was the ability of its inhabitants—elect souls and angels—to see what was transpiring on earth and in hell. What they would witness would, first, educate them about God's unfolding purposes, and consequently give them reasons to glorify God. Edwards would continue to espouse this view, as in "Miscellanies" nos. 776, 777, 778, 804 and 811 (to

---

23. "Miscellanies" no. 60, in WJE 13:229–33; no. 666, where Edwards uses Watts' *Essay toward the proof of a separate state of souls between death and resurrection* (London, 1732), and no. 710, in WJE 18:211–12, 335–39.

24. "Miscellanies" no. 952, 1121, and 1126, in WJE 20:210–22, 494, 496–97.

cite only a few roughly contemporaneous with *How Christians Are Come)*.²⁵

All of these themes, and many more, were to be incorporated into the "magnum opus," *A History of the Work of Redemption*, which Edwards later described in his letter to the trustees of the College of New Jersey but was unable to finish before he died.²⁶ In the first of a series of three notebooks that he compiled towards this project, for example, he sketched out his intention to discuss the separate state of souls in hades and heaven.²⁷ But these were to be subsumed in a grand vision of sacred time, or sacred times, from creation, to the Mosaic dispensation, to the gospel dispensation, to the millennium, to the day of judgment, and beyond, each age more glorious, more perfect, than the previous—a process to continue in heaven to eternity. A vision of the new heavens and a new earth were therefore behind the discourse that Edwards delivered in the spring of 1740, a vision that connected the work of conversion on earth—Christians coming into the church—and the simultaneous yet also future arrival of the church at the very throne of God.

The Sermon Series: A Summary

Sermon 1: How Christians Are Come to Mt. Sion

In his typical fashion, Edwards begins the sermon, and the series, with an explanation of the immediate scriptural context. He points out that one of the Apostle's purposes was earnestly to warn his hearers "to carefully avoid the ways of sin." The Apostle's "great

---

25. *The Works of Jonathan Edwards, Volume 18, The "Miscellanies," 501–832*, edited by Ava Chamberlain (New Haven: Yale University Press, 2000), 426–34, 505–7, 520–22. See also Sermon on Rev. 18:20, no. 277, Mar. 1733, with the Doctrine: "When the saints in glory shall see the wrath of God executed on ungodly men, it will be no occasion of grief to 'em, but of rejoicing." Published as *The End of the Wicked Contemplated by the Righteous*, in *Practical Sermons* (Edinburgh, 1778), 260–81; edited by Sereno E. Dwight, 6:466–85.

26. Edwards to Trustees, Oct. 19, 1757, in WJE 16:725–29.

27. "History of Redemption, Bk. I," WJEO Vol. 31.

argument" is that Christians have come to something far more glorious even than God's awesome and dreadful appearance when entering into covenant with his people at Mt. Sinai (complicating Doddridge's reading as quoted in the "Blank Bible"). That appearance caused upheaval not only in the earthly creation, in the blazing and quaking mountain, but also in the trembling hearts of God's people, and especially God's humble servant Moses.

Edwards reiterates the Apostle's message that Christians have now come to Mt. Zion, the heavenly Jerusalem. Because of the company that is there—God, angels, saints—it is even more awesome and fearful, and thus a greater restraint from sin, than was God's descent at Mt. Sinai. There is yet to come a more extensive shaking not only of the earthly realm, but also the heavens as well. Edwards will presently show that there is also something far greater, gracious, and delightful in that kingdom to which God's children have been brought, to cheer and rejoice their hearts. He points out that the kingdom to which Christians have come is described in the verses of the text under a "twofold representation": as both a place, and as one containing innumerable, glorious inhabitants.

Following the brief introduction, Edwards sets out the Method he intends to utilize for expositing the text. He will, in a series of sermons, explain each of the "particulars" of the Hebrews 12:22–24 passage. In this first sermon, he will show what it means when Christians are said to come to Mt. Sion; then, in subsequent preachings, he will speak on what it means that Christians are come to "the city of the living God," "to the heavenly Jerusalem," "to the general assembly of the church of the firstborn written in heaven," and so forth. And with each sermon, Edwards will not only explain but "improve" or apply the text to the lives of his hearers, whether to give understanding and exhortation to his Christian hearers, or to warn and invite those who may yet be "far off" from Christ.

Throughout the series of eight sermons, as he examines each of the "particulars" of the passage, Edwards continues to remind his hearers that these are all "privileges" to which Christians are come. As George Marsden has observed, "Edwards constantly urged his parishioners toward grand perspectives,"[28] and this series is no different, seeking to lift up the minds of his hearers to the things above.

In the development of his first proposition—"How Christians are come to Mt. Sion" (reflecting the spelling of the location in Hebrews)—Edwards explains the scriptural significance of the literal Mt. Sion of old, and here he gives a condensed, yet interesting account of the importance of Mt. Sion in the history of God's people. He then proceeds to explore the meaning of the scriptural text when it says that Christians "are come to Mt. Sion."

As mentioned in the sermon, this series was begun on a sacrament day, when the Lord's Supper was celebrated. Edwards has this in mind as he concludes, with application both "to those who are far off," as well as to those in the visible church. To the former, he asks that they consider their miserable condition, as though lost in the wilderness; but he asks that they also respond to Christ's call, to come to him. Christ invites sinners to come and eat and drink, to find nourishment and satisfaction for their souls. Edwards then asks professing Christians to examine how they are coming to God's house of worship—their grand, newly built edifice—and to the Lord's Table. Is it with an earnest desire after communion with God, and with solemnity and diligent attention? And is it with a joy and gladness befitting God's house, with an acknowledgment of the great privileges they have received? The questions imply that the preacher suspected that many were not.

Sermon 2: How Christians Are Come to the Heavenly Jerusalem

In the second "particular," Edwards shows how Christians are come to "the city of the living God, the heavenly Jerusalem." He begins by summarizing the biblical history of the city of Jerusalem. Jerusalem was, by its nature, a strong city that held out against the Israelites until it finally fell to David. It was then the city of David,

---

28. Marsden, *Jonathan Edwards: A Life*, 194.

the city of kings. After David took possession of the city he brought the ark of the covenant into it. Edwards notes that of all the locations in Israel, God chose to make his throne in Jerusalem. It was a magnificent city wherein God's people dwelt. Edwards recounts the history of the earthly Jerusalem to prepare his listeners for the parallel of where saints have come: the heavenly Jerusalem.

Edwards understands that Christians first come to the heavenly Jerusalem when they come into the church of Christ. Edwards sets forth five reasons why this is true. First, God's church is his Jerusalem, the antitype of the earthly Jerusalem, beautiful, the city of peace, strong, redeemed, and spiritual. The church is a heavenly society: in its qualities, and in its present and eventual abode. The head of the church is in heaven, as are the prophets and apostles and an innumerable company of martyrs. In the next installment of this series, Edwards will expand on the notion that Christians come to these righteous spirits made perfect when they come to Mt. Sion.

Next, Edwards explains to whom it is that Christians come when they come to the heavenly Jerusalem: namely, the living God. As God dwelt in the literal or temporal Jerusalem, so he lives in the heavenly Jerusalem, the divine city. It is in this place that God "does most remarkably manifest his distinguishing perfections and glory" (52). God dwells in the church in this world by gloriously manifesting God's self through redemption and providence for the church. But at the same time, Edwards explains, God also dwells in heaven, the "appointed place of the church's residence" (52).

Edwards makes application through two uses. The first Use is for the conviction of those who are not "aliens" to the heavenly city. The second Use is of exhortation to Christians to seek the city that is to come, and to seek the prosperity of that city.

Sermon 3: How Christians Are Come to an Innumerable Company of Angels

It is within the city of the living God, too, that believers find themselves in the presence of an "innumerable company of angels."

Edwards was not afraid to devote entire sermons to the subject of angels, and indeed had a robust angelology,[29] so it should not be surprising to see him use an entire part of this discourse to discuss the nature of these beings. Why is the number of angels considered to be "innumerable"? Edwards answers that the number of these native inhabitants of heaven is beyond conception. It seemed good to God to make their number vast for his glory. In addition, their service to God in ministering his providence requires a great multitude. The kingdom is so great, the design so various, and the souls so numerous, that a very great number of angels is required.

Edwards speculates there are likely more angels in heaven than humans on earth, but unlike humans who divide themselves over the smallest disagreement, the confirmed angels in heaven (those who did not rebel with Satan) are one in holy love. They are united in their heavenly home, in their conversation, in their fellowship, and in their business as ministering spirits.

Such an innumerable company, existing in such union, requires order and purpose. No matter their conversation, fellowship, or ministry, their head is Jesus Christ. Because Christ is the head of the angels, Christ is called the Archangel; Edwards even identifies Michael the Archangel as another manifestation of Christ. In addition, the angels are of differing orders and degrees, as we read in Colossians 1:16, "thrones, dominions, principalities, and powers."

Christians come to this innumerable company of angels "by the interest they have in the angels and the benefits they have by them" (59). Edwards understands that believers' interests in angels are fulfilled when Christ becomes their Savior, and they are married to Christ. United to the Lord of the angels, the angels become theirs.

---

29. See Amy Plantinga Pauw, "Where Theologians Fear to Tread," *Modern Theology* 16 (2000) 39–59; McClymond & McDermott, *The Theology of Jonathan Edwards*, 273–94; and Kenneth P. Minkema, "'If thou reckon right': Angels from John Calvin to Jonathan Edwards (via John Milton)," in *A Calvin Handbook*, edited by Carl Trueman and Bruce Gordon (New York: Oxford University Press, forthcoming).

Edwards cites the great benefit in having an interest in the angels, by their friendship and ministrations. They work for the temporal good of believers, to defend them and to deliver them. Angels have saved the saint from unseen sorrowful accidents, and they provide for temporal subsistence of the saints, as they did for Elijah. They comfort the saints at death, as they did for Christ. And it will be the angels who will be instrumental in ushering souls from the world and conducting the elect to heaven on the day of judgment.

Edwards puts forward five points of Application. First, the ministration of angels demonstrates the honor and blessedness of true Christians, that "they should be brought and added to such a glorious company" (62). It is an honor that God should appoint ministering spirits to have charge over the saints. Second, he suggests that such an honor may lead impenitent persons to a sense of their miserable condition. Instead of having the innumerable company of angels to their benefit, the angels are their adversaries. Like paradise after the fall, an angel bars their way. Edwards cites the destruction of Jerusalem (Ezekiel 9), the angel who opposed Balaam, and the destruction of Sennacherib's army, as examples of angelic service to resist evil humans. The third application explains why the angels in heaven rejoice at the conversion of a sinner: there is one added to their company, who can join them in praising God. This encourages God's people to bless God for the ministration of the angels, for it is also their ministration. Finally, Edwards issues a call to Christians to be of the same company with the angels, being "like a flame of fire in God's love and service" (67).

Sermon 4: How Christians Are Come to the General Assembly of the Church of the Firstborn Written in Heaven

In his exegesis of the fourth particular, Edwards begins with an exploration of the terminology that the Apostle used to describe the church of Christ. Edwards asks how the church can be called an "assembly," when in fact there are many congregations of saints scattered throughout the land, and in many different nations across the globe, at a great distance from each other. At an even greater and inconceivable distance are the saints in heaven. Together, they constitute "Christ mystical," assembled now on earth in a "spiritual sense," and later in heaven in a "literal" sense.

Then secondly, Edwards investigates the significance of the term "firstborn." Why is it that all the church of Christ is called "the church of the firstborn"? Edwards delves into Scripture to explore the "distinguishing privileges" that the sovereign God has lavished upon his children. Just as Christ as firstborn is set higher than the kings of the earth, and above all earthly thrones, so the saints, as his spouse, partake in the distinguished love and favor of the firstborn.

Thirdly, Edwards wants his audience to understand the Apostle's meaning when he says that their names "are written in heaven." This shows that their names are "from all eternity" written in God's book of decrees, as the elect. Also, they are enrolled "among the saints, the citizens of heaven."

In his explorations of the text, Edwards is at the same time reminding and encouraging his hearers of the greater reality that is theirs. He points out that the saints are daily departing to that great assembly that is now "actually there," and that the time will come when all are "actually assembled," and will forever join in the heavenly worship. It is an assembly that shall never disperse, and never hear a closing benediction to "Go in peace!"

In a brief Application, Edwards gives two Uses, one of Instruction, and one of Exhortation. In the Instruction, he encourages the saints to consider the privileges to which they are come or to which they are coming—illustrating his sense of the simultaneity of "now" time and "then" time. They are objects of Christ's dying love and his special delight. But he wants his hearers to consider yet another assembly, a gathering of those who are not heirs of "the free woman" of Genesis 21:10: those who are of the synagogue of Satan, and are "hasting to that great congregation."

In the closing exhortation, Edwards draws on the words of the Apostle to warn his hearers against a lifeless, sleepy way of attending worship, and to consider the purpose of the public, visible worshipping assemblies of God's people in this world. The Apostle warns elsewhere against a neglect and carelessness in this regard, and that public worship is to be attended with the utmost diligence and reverence, as those entering into the very presence of God, "considering the house of God as the gate of heaven." Edwards cites the example of Esau's folly of giving up his birthright for a bit of food, warning his hearers not to despise and sell such great privileges, or to trade such an inheritance for a short, momentary pleasure.

Sermon 5: How Christians Are Come to God the Judge of All

According to the Apostle, what immediately follows death in this world is judgment. Hebrews 9:27 declares, "It is appointed unto men once to die, but after this the judgment." There is no more solemn moment after death than to be brought to appear before God the Judge of all, to give an account of the life lived in this world, and then to hear the sentence pronounced determining one's eternal destiny. However, in this sermon the preacher reminds true Christians that coming to God the Judge of all is one of the privileges that they have through faith in the finished work of Jesus Christ.

In this fifth particular, Edwards explains "how Christians are come to God the Judge of all." The thought of coming to God as Judge of all can be as fearful as coming to Mt. Sinai where God gave Moses the law. When the Israelites came to Mt. Sinai it was a terrifying experience. The mountain trembled in the presence of its Maker. Smoke and lightning enveloped the mountain. The people dared not approach for fear of their lives. Even Moses was exceedingly afraid and trembled. God's fearsomeness is not limited to Mt. Sinai. The final verse of the twelfth chapter of Hebrews teaches that God remains a consuming fire (Heb. 12:29). However, Edwards reminds his congregation they do not come to Mt. Sinai, but rather to Mt. Zion. He labors here to encourage his people to understand that God's immovable and immutable justice is in their favor.

Edwards begins the sermon by distinguishing between the persons of the Trinity, identifying which person of the Trinity is "God the Judge of all." It could have been any one person of the Trinity, for they are all equally God. Our preacher points out, however, that the Hebrews passage distinguishes between God the Judge of all in v. 23, and Jesus the mediator of the new covenant in v. 24. As judge, the Father is the one who gives the law and the one who requires satisfaction of the law. By contrast, Jesus is the mediator of the new covenant: Jesus intercedes with his blood before God the Judge of all.

Edwards further emphasizes the distinction between the Father and the Son by examining the "economy," or roles, of the persons of the Trinity. Each person is appointed a role "in the management or transactions of divine providence towards [God's people]" (83). The Father, Son, and Holy Ghost agreed, in the covenant of redemption before the creation of the world, that the Father would give the law, and by doing so would be the defender and the judge of when and how it is satisfied. The Son would satisfy the law as the Mediator. The Holy Ghost would be the emissary of the two, accomplishing the success of the other two persons relative to the law.

Edwards is aware that some will object to the Father being God the Judge of all. Some will turn to Jesus' own teaching in John 5:22, "For the Father judgeth no man, but committed all judgment unto the Son." If the Father judgeth no man, how can the Father be God the Judge of all? Edwards answers that the Father's judgment on Mt. Sion does not fall on souls, but on the Son as the Mediator of the law. Edwards said as much in the contemporaneously written "Miscellanies" no. 813: "Christ is a fit person to judge between God and man, being a middle person between both the divine and human nature, and having manifested infinite regard both to the honor of God's majesty and justice, and to the welfare of mankind" (WJE 18:523). The Father accepts the satisfaction that Christ made, justifies Christ and acquits him. Edwards explains that when Christ does judge souls, he does so by delegation from the Father, as the Father's represented authority. Edwards sees

Christ representing the Father's authority in the giving of the law on Mt. Sinai. Christ, he argues, was the angel that spoke to Moses on Mt. Sinai (Acts 7:38).

In his "Discourse on the Trinity," Edwards reminds us that the Son of God is the divine "idea" of the Father, the Eternal Mind, and so is "the only begotten and dearly beloved Son of God. He is the eternal, necessary, perfect, substantial, and personal idea which God hath of himself."[30] The book of Hebrews asserts that Jesus is "the express image of his person" (Heb. 1:3). Edwards understands it is a necessary and glorious expression of the Trinity that the Son would represent the Father so intimately in the giving, defending, and satisfaction of the law.

Christians come to God the Judge of all, Edwards explains, as a privilege of the covenant of grace, that is, by the gospel. This privilege is proven by the context. Christians do not come to Mt. Sinai. They are privileged to come to Mt. Sion, as he has already explained, to an innumerable company of angels, and to the general assembly of the church. It is the Christian's privilege to come to God the Judge of all on Mt. Sion, not to the lawgiver and judge on Mt. Sinai. "What they are brought to at Mt. Sion are the privileges they are brought to by the gospel" (87).

The gospel does not convey the Christian merely to a milder or gentler God, or only to a milder or gentler aspect of God. Still very much—and necessarily—present is the same God of terror and strict justice revealed in the smoke, thunder, and shaking experienced on Mt. Sinai. But the gospel likewise portrays all the terrors of breaking the law that should have fallen on sinful humanity as assumed by Jesus the Mediator. When God the Judge of all brings down his gavel, it comes down on the Son. In this act of divine justice, God as Judge acquits the Christian of all guilt. It is for this reason that Edwards can view God the Judge of all sitting on Mt. Sion's throne of grace even as he sits on the old covenant's throne of justice revealed on Mt. Sinai. God is just, as well as the justifier of those that believe in Jesus (Rom. 3:26).

---

30. "Discourse on the Trinity," WJE 21:117.

The book of Hebrews encourages Christians to come boldly to the throne of grace so that they might find grace in times of need, and mercy for all time (Heb. 4:16). Christians come to the throne of God on Mt. Zion, not to satisfy or fulfill the law as on Mt. Sinai, but to "come to [Christ] as a judge to receive the reward of his obedience" (89). They come to the throne of grace, rather than to the throne of condemnation.

In the Application, Edwards reminds his congregation that this is a "matter of great consolation to true Christians, and terror and conviction to others" (89). Christians should find great consolation in the fact that "the strict, immovable and immutable justice of God is for them. Both law and gospel with united voice call for their happiness and eternal glory" (90). For true Christians, this doctrine is a matter of great consolation and rejoicing, and sure grounds for hopes of happiness. The foundation of their blessedness can no more be shaken than God's throne can be removed from its established and everlasting foundation. For those who are not true Christians, who scarcely perceive their danger, facing this Judge of all will bring despair and terror, encountering the One who is a consuming fire, and enduring the eternal execution of his just decree. The hope of the sinner is not to think that God will ever divest God's self of the character of a strict judge, or that one jot or tittle will by any means disappear from God's law. But Edwards shows them their need of a mediator, and that their only access and acceptance and favor with God is by the Mediator who has met the Law's demands.

Sermon 6: How Christians Are Come to the Spirits of Just Men Made Perfect

In the sixth sermon, Edwards begins by showing what the Scripture has to say about these "just" spirits, and then shows how Christians are said to come to these spirits. Edwards addresses three brief inquiries, supporting and confirming each answer using various Scripture passages. He asks: Who are these "spirits of just men made perfect"? How are these spirits designated "just men"? and, How are these departed spirits, now in heaven, said to be "made perfect"?

While the spirits of the departed saints are not yet in their highest and ultimate perfection, which is reserved for the resurrection, Edwards draws out the glories and excellencies of their state using a number of comparisons, showing from the Scripture how their knowing, serving, and enjoying God are now inconceivably more excellent and perfect. After all, they now see God, not through a glass, but face to face, and converse with him more immediately. Light and darkness are no longer mixed, but in that realm there is only light, as in a cloudless sky after the sun is risen. By describing the nature of divine emanation, Edwards wants to help his hearers set their minds on the things above.

Though the saints have not reached that perfect state, they are part of that same company, and have the promises and firstfruits of that glory in their souls. They are continually drawing nearer to that same perfection. Edwards uses scriptural and natural analogies to describe this state: saints drink of that same water that springs up unto everlasting life, and they have that seed within them that shoots forth its roots deeper and deeper, and is budding and blossoming, bearing fruit to eternal life.

Edwards concludes with an Application containing a Use of Instruction and a Use of Self-Examination. When Edwards was a young philosopher, he had denied the possibility of nothingness, defining it as that "which the sleeping rocks do dream of" (WJE 6:206). So, too, he here refutes the erroneous idea that the soul sleeps until the resurrection, showing how impossible it would be for "a state of perfect insensibility" to be called a state of perfection. How, he inquires, could a state of insensibility in any way be deemed a "privilege" for the saints? Furthermore, what acquaintance do the saints in heaven have with the church on earth? Would it make any sense that the heavenly society of saints and angels are ignorant of the state of the church on earth? In response, Edwards affirms his belief, as summarized above, that the company of heaven is able to view things on earth and in hell.

But most importantly, Edwards lays before his hearers their need for a strict examination of themselves, to know whether they belong to that heavenly society. When their spirits are separated from the body, will they go to the spirits of just men made perfect, or will they find themselves among the spirits in prison, perfect in wickedness and misery?

Sermon 7: How Christians Are Come to Jesus the Mediator of the New Covenant

In the next installment, Edwards seeks to demonstrate the links between Christ as Mediator and the new covenant—meaning the covenant of grace as opposed to the covenant of works. The covenant between God and fallen humanity requires a mediator, Edwards asserts, because the previous covenant was broken, and an offended God requires transacting with sinners through an intermediary. This new covenant, the covenant of grace, brings peace with God, reconciliation, deliverance, and a long list of other benefits. But the condition for claiming or receiving those benefits is faith in Christ. Yes, Edwards uses the term "condition" in describing the relation between faith and justification, but, as he defines the concept at great length and in great detail in his notebook on "Faith," he sees faith and justification as a symbiotic act that begins when the soul acquiesces in its need for a savior and "cleaves to" or "closes with" Christ as that Savior.[31] This covenant is "new" and more excellent by comparison with, and succeeding in order of time, the covenant given at Mt. Sinai, which restated or extended the covenant of works made with Adam. This Adamic-Sinaitic covenant, for Edwards, did not involve the possibility of obtaining heaven, only earth. As he states in "Miscellanies" no. 809, "Heaven is not the promise of the first covenant with Adam, but is only the promise of the covenant of grace and the inheritance which is alone by the purchase of Christ" (WJE 18:512–16).

---

31. "Faith" in *The Works of Jonathan Edwards, Volume 21, Writings on the Trinity, Grace and Faith*, edited by Sang Hyun Lee (New Haven: Yale University Press: 2003), 414–68.

Thus, the new covenant in Jesus Christ is far better. Christ is the mediator of this new covenant because he conveys it, along with its promises, from God to humanity, and confirms, receives, and bestows its blessings. Finally, Christians come to this Mediator by accepting him, uniting to him, and have communion with him in his benefits.

The Application is outlined, consisting only of statements of the major heads, meaning that Edwards extemporized on each or every point. Christless sinners should consider that they are "strangers" to the new covenant of promise, that the wrath of God abides on them, and that it would be "dreadful" to die in this state and have to appear before God. The concluding exhortation, therefore, is to come to Christ and trust in him: consider that he is a "fit" person for that role, and "what he will do for you in it."

Sermon 8: How Christians Are Come to the Blood of Sprinkling

At the beginning of this last sermon in the series, Edwards makes a brief return to where he started, to Mt. Sion, to remind his hearers that Mt. Sion of old was the mountain of the sanctuary, the place of sacrifice, where the blood of the sacrifice was sprinkled for cleansing. But looking back to the ninth chapter of Hebrews, Edwards shows that at the beginning of the nation of Israel, the blood of a sacrifice was also sprinkled upon the book, upon the people, and upon the tabernacle and its vessels, in confirmation of the old covenant, and to show that the blood of a sacrifice was necessary for the remission of sins. In the history of the people of Israel, Edwards argues, the many blood sacrifices also pointed to the need of a better sacrifice, to Christ himself, and to his blood that would establish God's new covenant, as well as cleanse and bring peace to the unclean soul.

In a series of five brief inquiries, Edwards analyzes the meaning of the final clause of the passage, to show the sufficiency and superiority of Christ's sprinkled blood. The inquiries he plans to pursue are: what blood is spoken of; why it is called "the blood of sprinkling"; what things Abel's blood "spoke"; how Christ's blood "speaks" better things than that of Abel; and, how Christians come to this blood of sprinkling.

Edwards also draws on the teaching of the book of Hebrews to this point, to show that Christ was appointed by God as high priest of the good things to come. Being sent on this errand by the Father, he willingly came to save poor sinners. Doing the Father's will was his delight. Says Edwards, this "was the thing that moved him to yield himself up to be slain. He loved us, and gave himself for us. [. . .] He had a great and earnest desire that sinners might obtain these good things, and to that end he spilt his blood. His laying down his life was but an expression of this desire: for this he prayed, a little before his blood was shed" (122).

The result for Christians, says Edwards, is that the satisfaction that Christ has made to divine justice by his blood is now imputed to them, and is looked upon as theirs, as if they themselves had paid the debt. Some of the good things that Christ's blood imputes are already bestowed upon them, and they are given a title to the rest, that they will soon possess.

Edwards concludes with a brief application, exhorting guilty sinners to come to the fountain of Christ's blood, to have it applied to their own hearts. With solemn warning, Edwards instructs his hearers that by accepting Christ, his blood will cry to God for their pardon. But if they despise and reject Christ, and tread his blood underfoot, it will call out for a more terrible vengeance than ever Abel's blood did. Edwards is likely echoing the earlier warning of the Apostle in Hebrews 10:29, "Of how much sorer punishment, suppose ye, shall he be thought worthy, who hath trodden under foot the Son of God, and hath counted the blood of the covenant, wherewith he was sanctified, an unholy thing?"

Winding up for his final conclusion, Edwards encourages his hearers to lay hold of Christ and his blood, for he has not only shed his blood but entered into glory with it, which provides the basis for those who believe in him to accompany him there. And "multitudes" have been cleansed and saved by this atoning blood. So Edwards ends on a conversionist note, imploring the unregenerate to come and have a part with these "happy souls."

SERMON 1

How Christians Are Come to Mt. Sion

Hebrews 12:22–24.

But ye are come unto Mt. Sion, and unto the city of the living God, the heavenly Jerusalem, and to an innumerable company of angels, to the general assembly and church of the firstborn, which are written in heaven, and to God the Judge of all, and to the spirits of just men made perfect, and to Jesus the mediator of the new covenant, and to the blood of sprinkling, that speaketh better things than that of Abel.

The Apostle had, in some of the preceding verses, been earnestly warning the Christian Hebrews or Jews, carefully to avoid the ways of sin. Vv. 13, etc., "And make straight paths for your feet, lest that which is lame be turned out of the way; but let it rather be healed. Follow peace with all men, and holiness, without which no man shall see the Lord: looking diligently lest any man fail of the grace of God; lest any root of bitterness springing up trouble you, and thereby many be defiled; lest there be any fornicator, or profane person, as Esau, who for one morsel of meat sold his birthright. For ye know how that afterward, when he would have inherited the blessing, he was rejected: for he found no place of repentance, though he sought it carefully with tears."

And the great argument that the Apostle makes use of to enforce this counsel, is that they were not come to Mt. Sinai, as their fathers were of old, but to Mt. Sion, "the heavenly Jerusalem," etc.; signifying that there is more at Mt. Sion to restrain us from sin, than there was at Mt. Sinai. There was a great deal to restrain from sin, that their fathers saw and heard when they came to Mt. Sinai. There was manifested the terrible majesty of God: for the mount burnt with fire, with blackness, and darkness and tempest, and the sound of the trumpet, and the voice of words giving forth the Ten Commands; which voice was so terrible, that the children of Israel entreated that the word should not be spoken any more: for they could not endure that which was commanded, and if so much as a beast touch the mountain it was to be stoned, or thrust through with a dart. And so terrible was the sight, that Moses himself said, "I exceedingly fear and quake," as 'tis said in the 18th, 19th, 20th [and] 21st verses. Here was a great deal to restrain and deter the children of Israel from sin, for they saw in what a dreadful manner the commands were given forth. They saw what a dreadful God it was that gave those commands, which might make 'em sensible how terrible his wrath would be against the breakers of the commands.

But yet the Apostle intimates that their fathers had not so much to restrain them from sin, at that material, earthly mountain, Mt. Sinai, as they have who are come to the spiritual, heavenly Mt. Sion. And therefore the Apostle, after he had declared what Christians were come to at Mt. Sion, in the conclusion at the 25th [and] 26th verses, he says: "See that ye refuse not him that speaketh. For if they escaped not who refused him that spake on earth, much more shall not we escape, if we turn away from him that speaketh from heaven: whose voice then shook the earth: but now he hath promised, saying, Yet once more I shake not the earth only, but also heaven."

In the three verses of the text, the state and circumstances of Christians is described under a twofold representation:

1. Of a place that they are come to. Here called Mt. Sion, "the city of the living God, the heavenly Jerusalem."

2. The inhabitants, or persons, there resident: "to an innumerable company of angels, to the general assembly and church of the firstborn, to God the Judge of all, to the spirits of just men made perfect, and to Jesus the mediator of the new covenant."

THE METHOD

in which I propose to discourse from these words, is to show, in order, in what sense Christians are said to be come to each of these: first, to show how Christians are come to Mt. Sion; second, how they are come to the city of the living God, the heavenly Jerusalem; third, how they are come to an innumerable company of angels; and so on, so that each particular may be taken as a distinct proposition, which I shall explain and improve. And therefore,

I. I would show how Christians may be said to be come to Mt. Sion.

In order to this, I would first show where the literal Mt. Sion was of old; and then show, in the second place, how Christians are come to Mt. Sion in a spiritual sense.

[*First.*] The literal Mt. Sion, or that which was of old called Mt. Sion, was a certain steep, rocky mountain or hill in the city of Jerusalem. The city of Jerusalem was not built upon a plain, but upon hills. It was compassed about with mountains on the outside; and not only so, but the city itself was built on hills, or mountains. There were several hills that it stood upon, and one of these was Mt. Sion, upon the top of which stood that part of the city of Jerusalem that is called the city of David. It was upon the top of this hill, that David's house or palace stood. It was the strongest part of all the city of Jerusalem. It seems to have been but little else but an high, solid, steep rock of difficult ascent, and was a strong fortress; and therefore it was the last part of the city of Jerusalem that was taken out of the hands of the Jebusites, and used to be called "the stronghold" and "the fort." We have an account of David's taking of it, II Sam. 5:6 and onward: "And the king and his men went to Jerusalem unto the Jebusites, the inhabitants of the land: which spake unto David, saying, Except thou take away the blind and the lame, thou shalt not come in hither: thinking, David cannot come in hither. Nevertheless, David took the stronghold of Zion: the same is the city of David. And David said on that day, Whosoever getteth up to the gutter, and smiteth the Jebusites, and the lame and the blind, that are hated of David's soul, he shall be chief and captain. Wherefore they said, The blind and the lame shall not come into the house. So David dwelt in the fort, and called it the city of David. And David built round about from Millo and inward."

Because David took it out of the hand of the Jebusites, and because his palace stood there, therefore it was called "the city of David." As 'tis said in the 9th verse, "David dwelt in the fort, and called it the city of David." And afterwards, David brought up the ark there into this Mt. Zion, or the city of David, and placed [it] in a tabernacle that he had pitched for it. We have a particular account of it in the next chapter [II Sam. 6].

So that after that, this Mt. Zion became the place of the sanctuary, the place of God's more immediate residence, and the special symbol of his presence, above all other parts of the land of Canaan. When the children first came out of Egypt and settled in Canaan, the ark was placed in Shiloh; but then it was taken captive by the Philistines, and when it was returned out of the land of the Philistines, it was placed at Kirjath-jearim. And till now, God had never revealed what city he had chosen to place his name there, and therefore it is said that the ark wandered in a temple and in a tabernacle. But now God, having revealed to David that Jerusalem was the place that he had chosen, David went to fetch up the ark from Kirjath-jearim to Jerusalem; but because Uzza was smitten, it was left a while at the house of Obed-edom, and then afterwards was brought up to Jerusalem, and was carried up unto Zion, or city of David, and placed in the tabernacle that David had pitched for it there. II Sam. 6:12, etc., "And it was told king David, saying, The Lord hath blessed the house of Obed-edom, and all that pertaineth unto him, because of the ark of God. So David went and brought up the ark of God from the house of Obed-edom into the city of David with gladness." After this, after the plague that there was for David's sin in numbering the people, God revealed by the appearance of the angel, at the threshing floor of Araunah the Jebusite, that it was his will that a temple should, in his son's days, be built to him there, where that threshing floor was; which was on Mt. Moriah, another hill in the city of Jerusalem, and the same hill where Abraham had formerly offered up Isaac his son.

And when the temple was built there, the ark was brought out of the city of David, which till then had been called Mt. Zion, and was brought into Mt. Moriah, and was placed there in the temple which Solomon had built. Which we have an account of, in the beginning of the 8th chapter of I Kings: "Then Solomon assembled the elders of Israel, and all the heads of the tribes, the chief of the fathers of the children of Israel, unto king Solomon in Jerusalem, that they might bring up the ark of the covenant of the Lord out of the city of David, which is Zion. And all the men of Israel assembled themselves unto king Solomon at the feast in the month Ethanim, which is the seventh month. And all the elders of Israel came, and the priests took up the ark." When the ark was brought away from the city of David, which till then had been called Mt. Sion, it seems to have brought away the name of Zion with it; so that Mt. Moriah, or the mountain on which the temple stood, seems after that to have been called by that name. Thus we find the prophets speaking of "the mountain of the temple," or "the mountain of the house of the Lord," often call[ing] it Mt. Sion. In the city of David, while the ark continued there, and afterwards on the mountain of the temple, when the ark was removed thither, the priests dwelt and officiated. And there, on their festivals and solemn occasions, the silver trumpets were blown, which Moses commanded 'em to make, and thither the congregation of the children of Israel used to be gathered together to worship God, as being the place that he had chosen. Agreeable to [the] 132nd Psalm, [vv.] 13–14: "For the Lord hath chosen Zion; he hath desired it for his habitation. This is my rest for ever: here will I dwell; for I have desired it"; and

Ps. 78:67–69, "Moreover he refused the tabernacle of Joseph, and chose not the tribe of Ephraim: But chose the tribe of Judah, the mount Zion which he loved. And he built his sanctuary like high palaces, like the earth which he hath established for ever."

I now proceed, in the
Second place, to show what is denoted by Christians being come to Mt. Sion.

Hereby seems to be signified, these several kinds of things they are brought to: viz., a joyful sound, a foundation, a fortress, a palace, a temple[,] and a throne.

1. That denotes the joyful sound that they hear. As I have already observed, the literal Mt. Sion of old was a place where the silver trumpet was blown, being sounded by the priests, to call the people to their solemn assemblies, and in token of joy at their great festivals. There was a joyful sound that the children of Israel used to hear from Mt. Sion.

So Christians do spiritually hear the joyful sound. They are brought to hear the sound of the gospel trumpet, the sweet sound of its glorious doctrines, its gracious invitations[,] and its precious promises.

The Apostle, in the context, put the Christian Hebrews in mind [of] what a dreadful sound their fathers heard at Mt. Sinai, when they heard those awful thunders, and that dreadful trumpet blast was sounded there exceeding loud, and such a terrible voice of words, that all the people in the camp trembled, and Moses himself "said, I exceedingly fear and quake." The sound was so terrible to 'em, that they could not endure it; the terribleness of it was too much for their feeble natures to hear; they entreated they might hear it no more.

But the Apostle says, we are not come to Mt. Sinai, to hear such a terrible sound; but we are come to Mt. Sion, where we may hear the pleasant sound from the silver trumpet of the gospel, a sound that need not fright us, but may cheer and rejoice our hearts. 'Tis not a sound that tends to drive us away with fear, but a voice that tends to draw and invite us; not a sound that we should need to desire that we may hear it no more, but a voice that we may hear with the greatest delight; not the sounds of awful threatenings, as that was at Mt. Sinai, but the sound of the most gracious promises.

At Mt. Sinai, the children of Israel heard the voice of God as a strict lawgiver, but Christians are brought to hear the voice of Christ as a Savior; whose voice, when the disciples heard it in his sermon on the mount, was a pleasant voice, not denouncing curses as the voice at Mt. Sinai did, but pronouncing blessings, saying, "Blessed are the poor in spirit: for theirs is the kingdom of heaven. Blessed are they that mourn: for they shall be comforted" [Matt. 5:3–4].

2. It denotes the foundation that Christians are come to, and that they build upon. As I have observed before, Mt. Sion, on which stood the city of David, was a rocky mountain, so as to be little else but a solid rock. So that David's house and the city of David that were built upon it, had a strong foundation: they were built on a rock. So historians give the same account of the mountain on which the temple was built. They say it was little else besides a solid rock.[1]

So Christians are spiritually built on a rock, as David's house, and city and the temple were. God has laid a strong foundation in the spiritual Mt. Sion, on which Christians build their hope and comport. Ps. 87:1, "His foundation is in the holy mountains." Those mountains of Zion, on which the city of David and temple were, were of old called "the holy mountains." Christians are come to Mt. Zion, as they are come to [a] sure foundation that God hath laid in Zion, spoken of in Is. 28:16; "Therefore, thus saith the Lord God, Behold, I lay in Zion for a foundation a stone, a tried stone, a precious corner stone, a sure foundation: he that believeth shall not make haste."

3. It denotes the strong fortress, that Christians are defended by. Zion, as I observed before, was an exceeding strong fortress;

---

1. See, for example, Matthew Henry, *An exposition of all the books of the Old and New Testament* (3rd ed., 6 vols.; London, 1725), 2:348: "This Temple is built firm, upon a Rock not to be taken down, as the Tabernacle of the O.T. was."

it was called the fort and "the stronghold" [II Sam. 5:7]. It was a place of great safety, easily defensible from an enemy because of its height, and because it was so steep and so difficult of access, and because of the matter of which it consisted, which was a rock; and therefore was a very apt figure of that strong defense which Christians have in Christ, who is their Rock and their fortress. He is the fort, whither they have fled for refuge. They have fled to Zion for safety from the awful things threatened at Sinai. Here they fly and are safe, and Sinai's wrath shall not touch 'em.

It is said of the godly person, that "He shall dwell on high: and his place of defense shall be the munitions of rocks," Is. 33:16.

It seems to be upon this account chiefly, that God in Scripture is so often called a Rock. As Deut. 32:4, "He is a Rock"; and v. 15, [Jeshurun] "lightly esteemed the Rock of his salvation," and innumerable other places. 'Tis in allusion to the fortresses in and about that land, which were usually built on high and steep rocks, such as Mt. Sion was, for the more safe defense from enemies.

4. It denotes the palace of the spiritual David that they come into. As you have heard, the palace of king David was built on the literal Mt. Sion of old. There he had his household, there was his family.

So Christians are come to the palace of the spiritual David, and are of his household or family. As in Eph. 2:19, "Now therefore ye are no more strangers and foreigners, but fellow citizens with the saints, and of the household of God." David's children dwelt with him in Mt. Sion; so Christians are Christ's children. Heb. 2:13, "Behold I and the children which God hath given me."

And they dwell on Mt. Sion in his house with him.

Christians belong to Christ's house, in two respects:

(1) As they are brought into his church, which is his household or family. The church itself is called the house of God, as being a spiritual house. I Pet. 2:5, "Ye also, as lively stones, are built up a spiritual house." Believers are expressly said to be the house of Christ. Heb. 3:6, "But Christ as a Son over his own house; whose house we are, if we hold fast the confidence and the rejoicing of the hope firm unto the end." And,

(2) As they belong to heaven, which is the glorious palace of Jesus Christ. This is their house. Though they now don't dwell in it, but are at a distance from it, yet they in a sense may be said to be come to it, because they are come to a title to it. It is the house that belongs to them, 'tis the house that was built for them, "prepared for them from the foundation of the world," as Matt. 25:34. This heavenly palace of Christ, is their proper home. They ben't in it now, but 'tis because they are from home. If they were at home, they would be actually there. 'Tis as certain that they shall be there in due time, as if they were already in possession. And therefore Christians, even while in this world, are said to sit together with Christ in heavenly places. Eph. 2:6, "and hath raised us up together, and made us sit together in heavenly places with him."

They are now of the same household or family, with those that are in heaven. Eph. 3:15, "of whom the whole family in heaven and earth are named." And as those that are of Christ's family are of the heavenly family; they eat of Christ's bread; they live upon the provision of his household; they are fed as his children at his table, of which there is a very lively representation at the Lord's Supper. They eat heaven's bread, or that bread which came down from heaven, and live upon the same excellent food that the saints and angels do in heaven. Ps. 78:25, "men did eat angels' food."

5. Hereby is denoted the temple that Christians are brought to. It has been observed that of old, Mt. Zion was the place of the sanctuary, that the city of David had the tabernacle and ark; and afterwards, Mt. Moriah, on which the temple was built, when the ark was brought into it, was called Mt. Sion. The same that is spiritually represented as the palace of the spiritual David, is otherwise represented as the temple of the great God. Both the church and heaven are called the temple of God. And Christians are brought to the temple in both respects: for they shall dwell in the house of the Lord forever. It is manifest that they shall be as "pillars in the temple of God," to "go no more out," Rev. 3:12.

6. Hereby is denoted the throne of grace that Christians are brought to. On Mt. Sion, David had his throne; and on the mount of the temple, God had {his throne}. God manifested himself very

differently at Mt. Sinai and Mt. Sion. At Mt. Sinai, he manifested himself as on a throne of strict justice, as a just lawgiver, having in readiness to revenge all violations of the law. But on Mt. Sion, God sat on the mercy seat between the cherubims of glory; he appeared there as in a throne of mercy, and not strict justice. So Christians are come to Mt. Sion, and not Mt. Sinai, as they are brought, through the mediation of Christ, to the mercy seat, where God sits and reigns in the kingdom of his love and grace. As in Heb. 4:16, "Let us therefore come boldly unto the throne of grace, that we may obtain mercy, and find grace to help in time of need."

APPLICATION.

Use [I] is of *Exhortation.*

First. To those that hitherto are far off, that never have been brought to Mt. Zion, that never have heard the joyful sound as such. Though they have heard the calls of the gospel externally, yet [they] never have heard them spiritually, understandingly and obediently; never have had the sound of the gospel make a joyful sound to them; never have built on that same foundation which God hath laid in Zion; never have fled for refuge to that strong fortress.

1. Consider how miserable a condition you are in, in this your distance from this holy mountain. You are wandering in a wilderness, in a naked, defenseless condition. You have no foundation better than the sand, for a dependence for your eternal welfare and happiness. And instead of being of the household of God, you are the children of the devil.

2. Consider the silver trumpet, that is sounded from Mt. Sion, is directed to you, to invite you to come thither also. As the silver trumpet sounded by the priests of old on the top of Mt. Sion, was to call all the people to come up there, and there to wait upon God in the solemn duties of his worship, and there to enjoy the privileges of God's people and to receive the blessing of God; so that silver trumpet of the gospel, that is sounded this day, and from time to time, is directed to you, to come to the spiritual, heavenly

Sermon 1

Mt. Sion. "Wisdom stands on the high places of the city, saying, Whoso is simple, let him turn in hither. Come, eat of my bread, and drink of the wine that I have mingled" [Prov. 9:3–5]. There is an invitation to you, to come into the palace of the spiritual David that dwells on Mt. Sion, that you may be one of his children, and that you may eat and drink at his table. You are invited this day, not only in the preaching of the Word, but Christ is showing you the excellent provision he has made for your soul, in that his table is spread for poor, sinful men this day, and furnished with that bread and wine that are symbols of the food of his children, representations of the meat and drink of angels.[2]

3. There is no other refuge from the dreadful wrath threatened at Mt. Sinai. 'Tis in vain to seek any other: there is no other fortress where you can have any safety; there is no other strong foundation where you can build. The gates of Zion stand open before you. There you may fly and be safe. There is a sure foundation laid, a precious corner stone.

Here is provision, in the house of the spiritual David, to feed and nourish, and strengthen and satisfy your soul; but there is no other food that can keep your poor soul alive.

I would mention three things, by way of *Direction*:

1. You had need first to be brought to Mt. Sinai, in order to your coming to Mt. Sion. That is God's usual manner, to deal with his spiritual Israel as he did with Israel of old: he first brought {them to Mt. Sinai, before bringing them to Mt. Sion}. So 'tis his manner, first to bring souls as it were to Mt. Sinai, to hear the voice of the law; to behold God, as on the throne of his strict justice, dreadfully denouncing awful threatenings and wrath against all such as are guilty of sin. He makes to see the lightnings; hear the thunders; feel the earthquakes; see the great fire of his wrath, burning to "the midst of heaven" [Deut. 4:11]; see the smoke and clouds and thick darkness with which God clothes himself: and thus to prepare them to come to Zion, to hear the pleasant voice {of the gospel}, to enter with joy into {his heavenly palaces}, to build on

---

2. This passage indicates that this sermon was delivered on a sacrament day.

that sure {foundation}, to come to the mercy seat {between the cherubims}, and to be feasted with the dainties of David's palace.

2. Inquire the way to Zion with your face thitherward. Make diligent inquiry after the way, that you may seek in the right way. You are a stranger to the way, and there are many bypaths; you had need, for your own safety, to inquire.

And seek in such a way that your face may ever be thitherward; i.e., be ever pressing forward, don't look back, don't let your face be set Zion-ward sometimes, and sometime another way. Let it always be that way, without ever looking back, without turning to the right hand or to the left.

3. And lastly, take heed that you don't mistake any other mountain for Mount Zion. There is great danger of such a mistake; persons are often guilty of it. Don't fly to some other refuge, instead of the true refuge. Take heed you don't build on some other foundation, instead of the sure {foundation of that rock}. Don't fly to the hills and the multitude of mountains, but to Mt. Zion alone. Many rest in other refuges, thinking they are safe; and many think they are got to Mt. Zion when they have not, and so perish forever: take heed of such a mistake.

Use II may be of *Direction* to visible Christians, how to behave themselves when they visibly come to Mt. Sion, as they do, especially in two things:

First. In coming to the house of God's public worship. When visible Christians come up to the house of God's public worship, this is something answerable to Israel of old, their coming to worship from all parts of the land of Canaan, to appear before God in Zion.

Second. When they come to the Lord's table. This is the nearest visible approach to God. Herein, we visibly come to the table of the spiritual David in his palace, and eat and drink there. Here we visibly partake of the great sacrifice, as the children of Israel were used {to eat of their sacrifices, [Deut. 12:27]}.

Let us, [with] these things [in mind], come to Zion in the following manner:

1. With earnest desire. How did the Psalmist cry [out for the living God, Ps. 42:2].

Let us come with thirsty appetites.

2. Let us come with solemnity and diligent attention. The greatest solemnity was required of old, of those that entered into Zion. To profane that place of God's residence, was esteemed a dreadful crime. 'Tis no less dreadful to profane Christian ordinances; yea, it brings greater guilt, as Christian ordinances are more excellent than Jewish ones.

3. Let us come to Zion with joy. So it becomes us to approach to our glorious King in Zion {with joy and gladness}; so it becomes us to acknowledge our great privilege in being allowed such an access. So the children of Israel were wont {to do, under the old covenant}; so it is foretold God's people should do in gospel times. Is. 35:10, "The ransomed of the Lord shall return, [and come to Zion with songs and everlasting joy upon their heads:] they shall obtain joy and gladness, and sorrow and sighing shall flee away."

SERMON 2

How Christians Are Come to the Heavenly Jerusalem

Hebrews 12:22–24.

[But ye are come unto mount Sion, and unto the city of the living God, the heavenly Jerusalem.]

I come now, in the

[II.] Second place, to show how Christians are come to "the city of the living God, the heavenly Jerusalem." For these two expressions in the text are put in opposition, as both signifying the same thing: the city of the living God is the heavenly Jerusalem. And here I would show:

First. What the literal or temporal Jerusalem of old was.

Second. How Christians are said to be come into the heavenly Jerusalem.

Third. How that heavenly Jerusalem is the city of the living God.

And then make some Improvement.

First. I would briefly show what {the literal or temporal Jerusalem of old was}. It was the metropolis or chief city of all the land of Israel. It was the royal city, or the city where the kings of the house of David dwelt. It was the chief city of the people of

Sermon 2

God. And it was a very great and populous city, and it had a great multitude of inhabitants. And it was the holy city: it often had that epithet given it in Scripture. It was the city that God chose out of all the tribes of Israel to place his name there, the place where he appointed the temple to be built, where God's ark and altar were placed, where alone it was lawful to offer sacrifice, and where all the males of the children of Israel were obliged to go and appear three times in the year.

And it was "the city of God" because there God dwelt; and "the city of the great king" and "the city of the living God," to distinguish it from the cities of the heathen round about that they looked upon sacred, as being dedicated to dumb, lifeless idols—as the great city Babylon was the city where was the temple of their idol, Bel [Is. 46:1]. And so it was common among the heathen: their principal cities were not only the cities of their kings, but the cities where their chief temples was built, which were supposed to be the chief residences of their gods, who were lifeless gods. But Jerusalem was the city of the living God.

And it was a very strong city, built chiefly on mountains, as was said before,[1] and encompassed with strong walls and many towers of defense.

And it was a very magnificent, beautiful city, the buildings stately and set in excellent order. Ps. 122:3, "Jerusalem is builded as a city compact together."

And it was a city where God's people dwelt and resorted, and where they were instructed in the law. And [it was] where the principal rulers and judges of the land resided. Ps. 122[:4–5], "Whither the tribes go up, the tribes of the Lord, unto the testimony of Israel, to give thanks unto the name of the Lord. For there are set thrones of judgment, the thrones of the house of David."

It is supposed to be the same that of old was called Salem, of which Melchizedek was king. It is indeed manifest by Ps. 76:1–2. The word "salem" signifies "peace," and the name "Melchizedek" signifies "King of righteousness." As the Apostle observes, Heb. 7:2, "To whom also Abraham gave a tenth part of all; first being

---

1. See the first sermon, above (41).

by interpretation King of righteousness, and after that also King of Salem, which is, King of peace."

It seems to have held out against idolatry longer than other parts of Canaan. For the land in general was then very corrupt.

It was afterward called "Jebus," as Judg. 19:10. It was one of the last places in the land of Canaan that was conquered by the children of Israel. Great part of it held out until David's time, by reason of its natural strength. He was the first that conquered it and redeemed [it] out of the hands of idolaters, and as it were out of the hands of idols, whom David called "the lame" and "the blind"; and took possession of it, and made it the royal city and brought the ark thither, though some part of it was inhabited before David, before he[2] carried the head of Goliath before [him]. And the king of Jerusalem is said to be slain by Joshua, Josh. 10:23. He was one of those five kings {of the Amorites whom Joshua defeated}.

I come now, in the

Second place, to show how Christians are come to the heavenly Jerusalem.

And in one word: they are so, in that they are come into the church of Christ. In this, they are fitly and properly said to be come to the heavenly Jerusalem, on the following accounts:

1. God's church is his Jerusalem. It is the antitype of Jerusalem of old. The church of God is in the Psalms and in the Prophets very often called by this name. It is called "the holy city," as Jerusalem was, Rev. 11:2. [It is called the] city which God hath chosen [I Kgs. 8:44]. 'Tis the royal city.

['Tis] a beautiful, magnificent, glorious city. [It is called,] "[The] perfection of beauty, The joy of the whole earth" [Lam. 2:15].

['Tis the city] in which reigns the spiritual Melchizedek.

It is the true Salem, or city of peace. There God "breaks the bow" [Ps. 46:9].

It is a strong city. Is. 26:1, "We have a strong city; salvation will God appoint for walls [and bulwarks]."

'Tis a city redeemed by the spiritual David.

2. MS: "this."

['Tis a city] where David has brought the head of the spiritual Goliath in triumph.

'Tis the city of spiritual feasts.

2. This church of God is an heavenly society, as it does in a sense come down from God out of heaven. As 'tis said of the New Jerusalem, which is the same with the heavenly Jerusalem, Rev. [21:2].

The church of God is a society of men that is not of the earth. The earth don't bring them forth. The men of this world are of the world, and speak of the world and savor the things that are of the world. They are of the first Adam, who "is of the earth," and is "earthy"; but the church is of the second Adam, who is "the Lord from heaven" [I Cor. 15:47].

The church of God is a distinct race or generation of men that are of a peculiar descent, different from the rest of the world. They are descended from God; they are of an heavenly race; they are derived from above.

The heathen feigned that their heroes [were from above].

Ps. 22:30, "A seed shall serve him; and it shall be accounted unto the Lord for a generation." That is, a seed should serve [God], and it should be accounted to the Lord for his posterity, or offspring, remotely and immediate.

The church is a distinct race that originally came from God, or from heaven.

The first founding of the church [was from God].

The means [were from God].

The prophets and other instruments {of God} were sent as it were from heaven.

Christ the great Savior is from heaven.

From thence is sent down the Holy Spirit.

There is their Father, there is their Savior, there is their elder brother, there is their portion.

3. They are a society that are heavenly in their qualities.

[They] have a heavenly nature.

[They are] a seed from heaven.

[They have] an unction from heaven.

All their graces are heavenly: [they have] heavenly love, humility, meekness, peace, zeal, praise.

[They are] heavenly in their walk and conversation. They are of an heavenly mind. Their desires are heavenly. They set their hearts on things above.

4. The place appointed for this church, as the proper place of its abode, is heaven. That is the place appointed for the church so much, that it belongs there properly. It don't belong to this world. As Christ tells the disciples, "Ye are not of the world, even as I am not of the world" [John 8:23]. Heaven is the metropolis, more magnificent and glorious.

5. The bigger part of it are actually in heaven.

All of past generations [of the church are in heaven].

There is the head of the church.

There are all the prophets {and} apostles.

[There is an] innumerable company of martyrs.

Those here below are but a small number in comparison, absent from them, as every nation has at all times a number that are abroad.

Therefore, the church is called the "Jerusalem which is above," Gal. 4:26. As such a nation may be said to dwell in such a country, though they are not all there, because there will be always a considerable number abroad.

Third. How 'tis the city of the living God.

1. 'Tis the city in which God dwells and does most remarkably manifest his distinguishing perfections and glory, and distinguished from all false gods.

He dwells in the church in this world. 'Tis the city where he dwells.

He gloriously manifests himself in it.

[He manifests himself] by the things that he hath done for the church. [He manifests himself in the] work of redemption {and in the work of} providence from time to time.

And he dwells in heaven, the appointed place of the church's residence.

2. In this, he manifests himself as the living God, in imputing life to his people. [He manifests himself as the] living God, and [the] life-giving God.³

APPLICATION.

Use I may be of *Conviction,* to convince those that are aliens from the commonwealth of Israel, and are not come to the heavenly Jerusalem, of their misery.

Use II may be of *Exhortation* to professing Christians, in two things:

First. To carry themselves as those that have no continuing city here, but that seek one that is to come. For as you have heard, the city you properly belong to is the Jerusalem that is above, the heavenly Jerusalem. If you are as you profess to be, you are not at home here, but belong to a society whose proper place of abode is heaven. Therefore, set your affections on those things as though you belonged here. Carry yourself as one that is on a journey.

Second. Seek the prosperity of this city of God.

---

3. JE leaves nearly all of L. 5 blank before resuming.

SERMON 3

How Christians Are Come to an Innumerable Company of Angels

Hebrews 12:22-24.

And to an innumerable company of angels.

I come now, in the

    III. [Third] place, to show Christians are come to an innumerable company of angels.

    There are three things that present themselves to be considered in this part of the text:

First. The number of the angels; and,

Second. Their society, whereby they are all one company; and,

Third. How Christians are come to this company.

    And the

    First thing that I would consider, is their numbers. They are said to be "innumerable." Both the good angels and the evil are in Scripture represented as exceeding numerous, but they are the good angels only that are spoken of in the text, when we are said to be come to "an innumerable company of angels." When they are said to be innumerable, it is not to be understood but that their number is limited, but their number is so great that it is beyond

Sermon 3

our conception. The holy Scriptures don't use superlative expressions lightly, to raise in us great ideas of things that are beyond what things are in themselves.

The angels are represented as a vast multitude in Dan. 7:10; "thousand thousands ministered unto him, and [...] ten thousand stood before him." And so it is in Rev. 5:11, "And I beheld, and I heard the voice of many angels round about the throne and the beasts and the elders: and the numbers of them were ten thousand times ten thousand, and thousands of thousands." And in many other places, they are represented as an exceeding great multitude. The angels are created as the native inhabitants of heaven; and it seemed good in the eyes of God, that as the highest heavens are the chief part of the universe, and doubtless a world of vastly greater extent than this lower world, that so its inhabitants should be very numerous. And God saw meet, for his more abundant declarative glory, to make an innumerable multitude of bright and glorious spirits, to [be] his constant attendants and ministers, and to praise his name. It is fit that the great king of heaven and earth should have a vast and inconceivable multitude of excellent, exalted creatures to be his attendants, and to surround his throne with their continual praises.

'Tis one thing wherein the glory and majesty of Christ's appearance at the day of judgment will consist, that he will appear attended with such vast multitudes of angels, when thousand thousands shall minister unto him, when he shall come with all the holy angels, the whole multitude of the heavenly hosts.

The services for which God created the angels, requires that there should be a very great multitude of them: for they are made to be the ministers of God's providence. But the dispensations of divine providence are so manifold and various, and of such vast extent, that a great number of ministers are requisite. The angels are especially intended to be ministers to Christ in the affair of his mediatorial kingdom and the work of redemption, and ministering spirits to his saints; but his work and kingdom is so great, the designs of it so many and various, and the souls so numerous, that a very great multitude of angels was requisite.

Second. The next thing that the text leads us to consider concerning the angels, is their union together into a society, whereby they are called a company.

And there are two things:

1. That union itself; and,

2. The order by which that union is regulated, maintained, and the principles of it answered.

1. That union itself, by which they [are] united. All this innumerable multitude of angels are united together. Though they are probably many more in number than there are men upon earth, yet 'tis not with them as 'tis with the inhabitants of this lower world, who are so exceedingly divided among themselves: but there is a strict union among them all.

They are many ways united together. They are united in holy love one to another, that is truly angelical, or worthy of the purity and the exaltation of the angelical nature, and worthy of their heavenly state. Love is called "the bond of perfectness" in Scripture. Col. 3:14, "and above all these things put on charity, which is the bond of perfectness."

The meaning of it is, that 'tis that bond by which holy societies are united together, so as to be perfectly one, that the society may be rendered complete by the union of all the parts.

The love of the angels is perfect. Every individual is in perfect charity and love with the whole, without the exception of any individuals, without any hatred, prejudices, envy, jealousy, discord[,] or misunderstanding whatsoever.

And they are united in cohabitation, dwelling all together in heaven.

And they are united in conversation. There is nothing to interrupt or hurt their conversation together, to keep 'em at a distance, or to hinder the most perfect freedom, or prevent the pleasantness of their conversation, or the usefulness of it, to hinder them in their assisting one another.

They are united in fellowship, or in a joint participation of good: all partaking of the same Spirit; all beholding the face of the same God; all having the happy influences of the same head that is set over them, even Jesus Christ; all partaking in the same blessedness.

They are united in business, all worshipping and praising the same God, worshipping in company by public worship. Thus we read that they "sang together," Job 38:7. So they are all ministering spirits; all do the work of the same Lord. And they are assisting to each other in this business, as we find they have been in the accounts that the Scriptures give us of their ministries time after time.

2. The other thing that concerns their union together into a society, is the order by which that union is regulated, maintained, and the ends of it answered. Union among a multitude is not to be upheld without order. If union ben't regulated in good order, or things are left in confusion, so union can't well subsist, nor the purpose of it be answered. If there ben't order, but disorder and confusion, this tends to discord and separation, and at last to enmity. Contention and confusion tend mutually to beget and to promote one another. And if union could be maintained without being regulated by good order, yet the ends of it could not be well answered. Therefore God, who is a God of order and not of confusion, has established a certain order among the angels. The Scriptures don't tell us particularly what that order is, but it plainly signifies that there is a certain order and subordination amongst the angels, whereby they became a regular society, a heavenly polity or political body with members of various place and degree. Thus they are all under one head that God has appointed over 'em, even Jesus Christ, God-man. They are all put under him. Heb. 1:6, "Again when he bringeth the first begotten into the world, he saith, And let all the angels of God worship him." And ch. 2:8, "Thou hast put all things in subjection under his feet. For in that he put all in subjection under him, he left nothing that is not put under him. But now we see not yet all things put under him." Eph. 1:21–23, "Far above all principality, and power, and might, and dominion, and every name that is named, not only in this world, but also in that which is to come: and hath put all things under his feet, and

gave him to be the head over all things to the church, which is his body, the fullness of him that filleth all in all."

Christ himself is often called "the angel of the Lord"; Gen. 22:15, "And the angel of the Lord called out of heaven." And "the angel of God's presence," Is. 63:9. And the angel of the covenant; Mal. 3:1, "Behold, I will send my messenger, and he shall prepare the way before me: and the Lord, whom ye seek, shall suddenly come to his temple, even the messenger of the covenant." An Angel; Ex. 23:20, "Behold, I send an Angel." And God's angel [Num. 22:22], by way of eminence. [And] "the angel"; Hos. 12:4, "He had power over the angel."

And because he is the head of all the angels, he is called the Archangel. Jude 9, "Michael the archangel," by which is meant Christ, as appears by the place cited—[he] is called "the Lord," Zech. 3:2—and by Dan. 12:1, "And at that time shall Michael stand up, the great prince which standeth for the children of thy people: and there shall be a time of trouble, such as never was since there was a nation even to that same time: and at that time thy people shall be delivered, every one that shall be found written in the book"; and 10:21, "[there is none that holdest with me in these things, but Michael your prince]."

And under Christ, some of the created angels are of one order and degree, and others of another. Hence those different appellations of "thrones, dominions, principalities, and powers," Col. 1:16. Which seems[1] to denote distinct places and degrees of divinity and power among the angels.

And thus the innumerable multitude of angels are called a company in the text, as they are all united together into a one regular, excellent society.

I now proceed, in the

Third [place], to show how Christians are come to this innumerable company of angels.

They are so principally in two things:

---

1. MS: "seemd."

Sermon 3

1. In being received to be some of the society or company that they are of; and,

2. In that interest that they are brought to have in them.

1. They may be said to be come to the innumerable company of angels, from being received.[2]

2. Christians may be said to be come to this innumerable company of angels by the interest they have in the angels and the benefits they have by them. True Christians are come to have a kind of propriety in the angels, so that they are called "their angels." Matt. 18:10, "Take heed that ye despise not one of these little ones; for I say unto you, That in heaven their angels do always behold the face of my Father which is in heaven."

When Christ becomes theirs, his angels become theirs. As I Cor. 3:22–23, "Whether Paul, or Apollos, or Cephas, or the world, or life, or death, or things present, or things to come; all are yours; and ye are Christ's; and Christ is God's."

When a person is spiritually married unto Christ, the Lord of the angels, the angels, who are as servants and attendants, of course become theirs. And the saints have an interest in them, not only by a kind of propriety, but by affection. The angels are united to the saints in friendship: they love those that they are sensible Christ died for. They are represented as Christ's friends in the 15th [chapter] of Luke, v. 6. And thus Lot and Abraham entertained angels as their friends.

And the saints have great benefit by their friendship and ministrations. Heb. 1:14, "Are they not all ministering spirits, sent forth to minister to [them] that shall be the heirs of salvation?"

The Scriptures represent as though God made use of the ministration of angels to promote their temporal good, to defend 'em from temporal enemies, and to deliver 'em from temporal calamities. Ps. 34:6–7, "This poor man cried and the Lord heard him, and delivered him out of all his troubles. The angel of the Lord encampeth round about them that fear him, and delivereth them."

---

2. Edwards left the remainder of L. 10v., the equivalent of approximately ten lines, blank, perhaps signaling his intention to complete the point extemporaneously.

The expression of "encamping round about" the saints, alludes to soldiers encamping in the field when they go forth to war, when the armed guard of a prince will encamp round about him in the night to protect him, that no enemy may approach. As [is] said of Solomon's bed, in Cant. 3:7–8; again, Ps. 91:10–11, "There shall no evil befall thee, neither shall any plague come nigh thy dwelling. For he shall give his angels charge over thee, to keep thee in all thy ways."

By this, it appears that the true saints have the guardianship of angels when they go to and fro in the way of their duty, to take care of them and to save from harm that might befall them; and doubtless many a time save them from unseen, sorrowful accidents and death, when they are not aware of it. [Angels] are often the instruments of their deliverance when in eminent danger, as angels were sent to save Lot out of Sodom when it was going to be destroyed—though they don't commonly deliver in so extraordinary a manner.

And there is also reason to believe that the ministry of angels is made use of in some respect or other, in providing for the temporal subsistence of the saints, as of old God made use of. We read of an angel's taking care to feed Elijah in an extraordinary manner. I Kgs. 19:4–8, "But he himself went a day's journey into the wilderness, and came and sat down under a juniper tree: and he requested for himself that he might die; and said, It is enough; now, O Lord, take away my life; for I am not better than my fathers. And as he lay and slept under a juniper tree, behold, then an angel touched him, and said unto him, Arise and eat. And he looked, and, behold, there was a cake baken on the coals, and a cruse of water at his head. And he did eat and drink, and laid him down again. And the angel of the Lord came again the second time, and touched him, and said, Arise and eat; because the journey *is* too great for thee. And he arose, and did eat and drink, and went in the strength of that meat forty days and forty nights unto Horeb the mount of God."

So angels are improved to prosper the saints in their concerns, when they perceive it not. As Gen. 24:7, "The Lord God of

Sermon 3

heaven, which took me from my father's house, and from the land of my kindred, and which spake unto me, and that sware unto me, saying, Unto thy seed will I give this land; he shall send his angel before thee, and thou shalt take a wife unto my son from thence."

And they are also doubtless many ways instrumental of the good of their souls, directing them in the way that they should go. [As] Peter, Acts 10:3, etc.,

> He saw in a vision evidently about the ninth hour of the day an angel of God coming in to him, and saying unto him, Cornelius. And when he looked on him, he was afraid, and said, What is it, Lord? And he said unto him, Thy prayers and thine alms are come up for a memorial before God. And now send men to Joppa, and call for one Simon, whose surname is Peter: he lodgeth with one Simon a tanner, whose house is by the sea side: he shall tell thee what thou oughtest to do. And when the angel which spake unto Cornelius was departed, he called two of his household servants, and a devout soldier of them that waited on him continually; and when he had declared all these things unto them, he sent them to Joppa.

Comforting them {in death}. As Christ, Luke 22:43, "And there appeared an angel unto him from heaven strengthening him." [Angels carried Lazarus to Abraham's bosom] at death, Luke 16:22.

Though [angels are] not commonly [used] in such an extraordinary way.

At the day of judgment, [angels will be instrumental in] separating [souls] from the world, conducting [the elect to heaven]. Matt. 13:39, etc., "The enemy that sowed them is the devil; the harvest is the end of the world; and the reapers are the angels"; and 24:30–31, "And then shall appear the sign of the Son of man in heaven: and then shall all the tribes of the earth mourn, and they shall see the Son of man coming in the clouds of heaven with power and great glory. And he shall send his angels with a great sound of a trumpet, and they shall gather together his elect from the four winds, from one end of heaven to the other."

APPLICATION.

[I.] This shows the great honor and blessedness of true Christians, that they, though worms of the dust, should be brought and added to such a glorious company, and should be joined with them to fill up the vacancy made among them by the sin of those that fell; that they, though by nature they are vile creatures, polluted, hateful[,] hell-deserving sinners, should be received into the fellowship of angels, to be companions with them, to be united with them in love, to be received among them as their dear friends, and to join with them in their work, to praise God forever with them and to partake with them in their blessedness. And not only so, but that they should be admitted to such an interest in them that they should become their angels, and be so called by Christ, the Lord of angels.

And that God should appoint them to be ministering spirits to them, and should give them charge concerning them to keep them in all their ways, to go with them wherever they go, as it were to bear them up in their hands lest at any time they should dash their foot against a stone, and should command them to pitch their tents round about them.

And at last, when they come to die, should have a special charge concerning them, to stand round about their dying bed as a guard to them and to receive their departing souls, and conduct them into the paradise of God, where they shall be presented by them to the Lord Jesus Christ that has bought them, and where they shall dwell forever with angels in those glorious mansions which were lost by the angels that fell. So shall [they] re-people heaven, which was in a measure emptied of its inhabitants by the fall of the angels.

This shows the great love of God to the saints, who begrutches nothing to 'em as too good for 'em, esteems none of his creatures too honorable and glorious for their society; yea, to be made ministers to them, to be subservient to their good, nor too happy for them to be sharers with. This shows the safety of such as are true Christians from all evil, in that [God] takes such special care

Sermon 3

to defend them as to give such mighty spirits charge concerning them, to watch over them and keep wherever they are. This may encourage the saints the more constantly and earnestly to resist Satan, in that though they have evil angels that tempt them and are continually seek[ing] their mischief, yet they have good angels to be on their side, to strengthen and defend them, to withstand those evil spirits.

II. This may lead all impenitent persons to a sense of the miserable condition that they are in, who are not come to this innumerable company of angels, are not looked upon fit to be joined to that glorious society, to partake of that honor and happiness, but rejected with the greatest abhorrence, as most unworthy of any such privilege; who have not the protection and ministry of angels, have no such heavenly guard to attend them when they lay themselves down to sleep, have not their safe conduct as they go from place to place.

But on the contrary, have 'em for their adversaries: for they are enemies to God's and Christ's enemies, and instead of joyfully attending on them and conducting them to blessedness, stand ready as it were with a flaming sword to keep them off and drive them [out].

As when Adam sinned: the angels, that before were his friends, drove him out of paradise, and stood with a flaming sword to keep the way of the tree of life, that he might not come nigh.

God makes use of the ministry of the angels for the good of his children, but on the contrary sends forth his angels to punish and destroy his enemies. Thus he sent forth his angels to destroy the sinners of Sodom and Gomorrah; and much more will he send them forth to destroy gospel sinners: for "it shall be more tolerable for the land of Sodom and Gomorrah in the day of judgment, than for that city" [Matt. 10:15].

Let us see how God improved the angels in destroying Jerusalem of old, though it had been the beloved chosen city. Ezek. 9, at the beginning:

> He cried also in mine ears with a loud voice, saying,
> Cause them that have charge over the city to draw near,

even every man with his destroying weapon in his hand. And, behold, six men came from the way of the higher gate, which lieth toward the north, and every man a slaughter weapon in his hand; and one man among them was clothed with linen, with a writer's inkhorn by his side: and they went in, and stood beside the brasen altar. And the glory of the God of Israel was gone up from the cherub, whereupon he was, to the threshold of the house. And he called to the man clothed with linen, which had the writer's inkhorn by his side; and the Lord said unto him, Go through the midst of the city, through the midst of Jerusalem, and set a mark upon the foreheads of the men that sigh and that cry for all the abominations that be done in the midst thereof. And to the others he said in mine hearing, Go ye after him through the city, and smite: let not your eye spare, neither have ye pity: slay utterly old and young, both maids, and little children, and women: but come not near any man upon whom is the mark; and begin at my sanctuary. Then they began at the ancient men which were before the house. And he said unto them, Defile the house, and fill the courts with the slain: go ye forth. And they went forth, and slew in the city.

When wicked men go about in pursuit of the world, seeking after the objects of their lusts, God don't send his angels to keep 'em in their ways, but to oppose them as it were with a drawn sword in their hands. As he sent his angel to oppose Balaam, when he went after his covetousness and "loved the wages of unrighteousness" [II Pet. 2:15]. Numbers, 22nd chapter, [vv.] 21, etc.:

And Balaam rose up in the morning, and saddled his ass, and went with the princes of Moab. And God's anger was kindled because he went: and the angel of the Lord stood in the way for an adversary against him. Now he was riding upon his ass, and his two servants were with him. And the ass saw the angel of the Lord standing in the way, and his sword drawn in his hand: and the ass turned aside out of the way, and went into the field: and Balaam smote the ass, to turn her into the way. But the angel of the Lord stood in a path of the vineyards, a wall being on this side, and a wall on that side. And when the ass saw the angel of the Lord, she thrust herself unto the wall, and crushed Balaam's foot against the wall: and he smote her again. And the angel of the Lord went further, and stood in a narrow place, where was no way to turn either to the right hand or to the left. And when the ass saw the angel of the Lord, she fell down under Balaam: and Balaam's anger was kindled, and he smote the ass with a staff. And the Lord opened the mouth of the ass, and she said unto Balaam, What have I done unto thee, that thou hast smitten me these three times? And Balaam said unto the ass, Because thou hast mocked me: I would there were a sword in mine hand, for now would I kill thee. And the ass said unto Balaam, Am not I thine ass, upon which thou hast ridden ever since I was thine unto this day? was I ever wont to do so unto thee? and he said, Nay. Then the Lord opened the eyes of Balaam, and he saw the angel of the Lord standing in the way, and his sword drawn in his hand: and he bowed down his head, and fell flat on his face. And the angel of the Lord said unto him, Wherefore hast thou smitten thine ass these three times? behold, I went out to withstand thee, because thy way is perverse before me: and the ass saw me, and turned from me these three times: unless she had turned from me, surely now also I had slain thee, and saved her alive. And Balaam said unto the angel of the Lord, I have sinned; for I knew not that thou stoodest in the way against me: now therefore, if it displease thee, I will get me back again. And the angel of the Lord said unto Balaam, Go with the men: but only the word that I shall speak unto thee, that thou shalt speak. So Balaam went with the princes of Balak.

And what fearful destruction did God make of the army of Sennacherib. II Kgs. 19:35, "And it came to pass that night, that the angel of the Lord went out, and smote in the camp of the Assyrians an hundred fourscore and five thousand: and when they arose early in the morning, behold, they *were* all dead corpses."

And what was the service that the angel of the Lord had to do with respect to Herod, when his heart was lifted up with pride?

[Acts 12:23]. These things show how different the ministry of angels is concerning the wicked, from what it is about the godly.

And wicked men, instead of having angels to attend them as their friends, as their constant guard, have devils to attend them and lead them into snares, to deceive and delude them and lay stumbling blocks in their ways; and many of them are left to Satan's power and influence, and are given up to it. That curse is fulfilled upon them, Ps. 109:6, "Set thou a wicked man over him: [and let Satan stand at his right hand]."

Many men are strangely under the power of the devil, who leads 'em captive at his will: and the reason is, God don't protect them, but has given up 'em to the devil. These considerations may well lead all Christless persons to consider the very miserable state they are in.

III. Hence we may learn one reason why the angels in [heaven] rejoice at the conversion of a sinner. Luke 15:10, "Likewise, I say unto you, there is joy in the presence of the angels of God over one sinner that repenteth." For when a sinner is so converted, there is one added to their company, to join with them and assist them in their work of worshipping and praising God and the Lamb. There is one then gathered to the same head that they are under, and whom they love with ardent affection. And the convert, as he appears then to be one of Christ's, is received by them into their esteem and love.

IV. Hence God's people ought to bless God for the ministration of angels. Christians, when they are well satisfied of their good estate, are wont to bless God for his grace and the holy influences of his Spirit, that he has e'en enlightened them, and that he has forgiven their sins and helped 'em against temptations. And Christians are wont also to bless God for temporal mercies. But 'tis to be feared that this great mercy, this remarkable token of God's favor, his giving them the ministration of angels to encamp round about them, to guard and protect them, and to go with them to keep in their ways, is very much forgotten in their thanksgivings; though it be so great an honor that God puts upon poor worms of the dust, and though the benefits they receive by the help of these blessed and glorious spirits, that Christ sends to minister to them, is very great. If a prince should treat any one of his mean subjects so much as a peculiar favorite as to appoint a strong guard to attend him and defend him on his way from any mischief, would it not be ingratitude if he should forget to thank his prince for it? Much more is [it] ungrateful for poor worms of the dust not to give God thanks when he appoints glorious angels to attend them, and minister to them.

V. If Christians are come to be of the same company with the angels, then they ought, as far as in them lies, to be like them, that they may be fit for such a privilege and station. They should seek that they may be more like a flame of fire in God's love and service, as they are, and should employ themselves more as they do in praising and glorifying God. And seeing the time is drawing nigh when they hope to be actually with them in these their heavenly exercises, they should labor that they [be] more and more assimilated to them, that at last they may [be] made the more welcome into their assembly, and may have the more abundant entrance ministered to them into their habitation.

SERMON 4

How Christians Are Come to the General Assembly of the Church of the Firstborn Written in Heaven

Hebrews 12:22–24.

To the general assembly of the church of the firstborn, which are written in heaven.

I come now to show, in the

[IV.] Fourth place, how Christians are said to come to the general assembly and church of the firstborn, which are written in heaven.[1]

That which is here called "the general assembly of the church of the firstborn," is the whole invisible church of Christ, consisting both of living and departed saints, or containing both that part of the church which is in the earth, and also that which is in heaven; or, in one word, the whole mystical body of Christ. There are many particular assemblies of Christians, multitudes of worshipping congregations of God's people; and there are provincial and national churches; and there is the church universal, which, in the ordinary acceptation of the phrase, signifies the whole church

---

1. Edwards' shorthand notation here reads: "The doctrinal part [. . .] the second time, 1740."

militant upon earth. But yet this don't contain the whole church of Christ, and indeed is but a small part of the church in its largest extent, as consisting of the saints both in heaven and earth. And this is what is called "the general assembly of the church of the firstborn, that are written in heaven."

Here, several things come under consideration:

First. Why [the] church of Christ, in this sense of it, is called an "assembly."

Second. Why it is called "the church of the firstborn."

Third. How they are said to be "written in heaven."

First. We are to consider why the church of Christ, as consisting of the saints in heaven and earth, is called an assembly. They are at a great distance one from another. The different parts of the church on earth, are very much separated; they are dispersed through great part of the world, among various nations. They never assemble together into one place: so far from that, that many parts of the church of Christ on earth never so much as know of many other parts of it.

But these are not at so great a distance one from another, as the saints in heaven are distant from the saints on earth. They dwell in a world that is invisible, and at an inconceivable distance from us. How then are they spoken of as one assembly, as though they were all assembled together?

It seems to be upon two accounts: partly on account of that assembling of them together, which is now; and partly on account of what shall be hereafter.

1. They are now all assembled together in a spiritual sense. While they were in a natural state, and under sin, they were in a state of separation from God, and distance one from another, being alienated in their minds and enemies both to God and men, and divided by contrary interests. But in Christ Jesus, they are all brought together: he hath gathered them together in one. They are all brought together as it were from the utmost ends of the earth under one head, Jesus Christ. They are brought into his kingdom and into his house, and have fellowship one with another. There is

one God, one Lord Jesus Christ, one Spirit, and they are "called in one hope of their calling" [Eph. 4:4]; they are united in affection, so far as they are known one to another. Thus the saints on earth, are one assembly with those in heaven. They are all one mystical body of Christ, and all have fellowship in the same Spirit, the same business and the same inheritance.

2. Hereafter they shall all, in a literal sense, be assembled together. The place of the assembly is in heaven, as the place of the assembly of Israel of old was the temple.

And that they are daily assembling, going up every day. There is a great assembly there already: much the bigger part of the church that is now in being, is actually there, and others are going there; all of them are travelling that way: and the time will soon come when they will all be together. So that all the saints, both in heaven and earth, are either actually assembled in the place of their general assembly, or else are in their way thither, so that they are all properly said to belong to the same assembly.

In Israel of old, all the males above a certain age were wont, three times in the year, to meet together in one assembly at the temple [Ex. 23:17]; and hence the whole nation were called "the congregation of the Lord," or God's assembly. And those minors that stayed at home, were said to belong to the congregation of Israel, though they had never yet assembled with others, being yet in a state of infancy. So 'tis with that part of the church that is on earth: they are as it were in a state of infancy. But when that is past, they shall be assembled in the heavenly temple with the rest of the congregation of Israel, and then they shall abide together in that assembled state to all eternity, forever joining together in the heavenly worship. 'Tis an assembly that never shall break up.

I now proceed, in the

Second place, to consider why the saints are called the firstborn. For when the church is called the church of the firstborn, 'tis not meant only that they are the church of Christ, who is the firstborn of every creature [Col. 1:15]. For the word "firstborn," in the original, is in the plural number; so that 'tis the saints, of which the church consists, that are called the firstborn.

In order to understand this, we must first consider how it was with the firstborn sons of old; and then show what that is that corresponds with it in the saints, of which the church of Christ consists.

1. As concerning the firstborn sons of old.

(1) The firstborn sons of the children of Israel, were privileged with a greater share of their fathers' inheritance, than the rest of the children. They had a double portion by God's appointment. As Deut. 21:17, "But he shall acknowledge the son of the hated for the firstborn, by giving him a double portion of all that he hath: for he is the beginning of his strength; the right of the firstborn is his."

(2) Those who were possessed of any peculiar office or dignity that was hereditary, it descended to the firstborn. So the firstborn sons of their princes, were heirs to the crowns of their fathers, unless there was some special interposition of heaven to alter it. So the firstborn son of the high priest was high priest after his father, by inheritance.

(3) The firstborn was God's part.

(4) In the times of the patriarchs, in every family, the firstborn son was the priest of the family, by inheritance. Thus it was, till God separated the tribe of Levi, and the family of Aaron, and then the priesthood was confined to that family. But before that, every family or house had a priest of its own, who were the firstborn sons. And therefore, when God separated the Levites, he took them, instead of the firstborn sons. Num. 3:12, "And I, behold, I have taken the Levites from among the children of Israel instead of all the firstborn that openeth the matrice among the children of Israel: therefore the firstborn shall be mine." And hence when God gave orders to Moses for the offering sacrifices in the congregation of Israel, before the Levites were separated and consecrated to that service, we are told that Moses set young men of the children of Israel to do it. Ex. 24:5, "And he sent young men of the children of Israel, which offered burnt offerings, and sacrificed peace offerings of oxen unto the Lord." These young men were doubtless their

firstborn sons, who were the priests of Israel, before the separation of the Levites.

And hence it is partly, that Esau's act in selling his birthright, is spoken of as such an instance of profaneness in him. It was profaneness on two accounts, viz., both because the blessing of Abraham belonged to his birthright, and also the priesthood: for he being the firstborn, the priesthood of the family belonged to him by his birthright, which priesthood was a sacred thing, a privilege which he ought highly to have valued as an holy thing. And it showed his horrid contempt of that which [is] sacred and holy, to sell it for a morsel of meat, to satisfy a carnal appetite. These were the privileges that the firstborn of old had, above other children.

[2.] From whence we may suppose, that the saints in the text are called the firstborn, on account of the peculiar privileges which they have above the rest of God's creatures, in like manner as he that had the birthright of old, had peculiar privileges above the rest of the children. God has been pleased to give the saints the birthright. The birthright of old, or the privilege ordinarily annexed to the privilege of birth, did not always go according to priority of natural birth; but sometimes God, who is the sovereign disposer of all, gave it to the youngest child. Thus he gave the birthright to Isaac, and appointed him to be Abraham's heir; though he was younger than Ishmael, he ordered that Hagar and Ishmael should be cast out, to make way for it.

So the saints are God's firstborn, by reason of the distinguishing privileges which a sovereign God hath given them, above others of his creatures. And when they are called the firstborn, it must be with respect either to other men, or to the angels.

(1) God has given 'em peculiar privileges above other men. Other men, though they are indeed God's enemies, and will be treated as such at last, yet they are some of God's creatures; and so we find that they are in some respect called his "sons" in Scripture, Acts 17:28. And the saints are called "the firstborn," in the same manner as they are called "the firstfruits of God's creatures," Jas. 1:18, Rev. 14:4.

Sermon 4

The kings of the earth are, in the 82nd Psalm, 6th verse, called "the children of the most High": "I said, Ye are gods; and all of you children of the most High." Though in the same psalm, they are spoken of as very wicked men.

Other men, being in some respect God's children, therefore God gives 'em all portions. But as of old, the firstborn son had a double portion. So the saints have the best portions.

Other men have their portion in this life. God gives them their portion in those things that he values but very little. Some of 'em have great estates, some are advanced to honor, some live in pleasure.

But God has some better thing for the saints. The firstborn are heirs of a better inheritance, than such things as those.

We read of Abraham, that as to the rest of his sons, besides Isaac, he gave 'em gifts, and sent them away from Isaac his son, eastward, into the east country, Gen. 25:6–7, but that he gave all that he had unto Isaac. So God deals with others of the children of men: he gives 'em portions and sends 'em away. They have, every one, their part of good things in their life, and God sends 'em away from him. But his first are his heirs: he won't send them away; they shall dwell with him forever. Christ does by his church, as Elkanah did by Hannah, his beloved wife. I Sam. 1:4–5,[2] "And when the time was that Elkanah offered, he gave to Peninnah his wife, and to all her sons and her daughters, portions: but unto Hannah he gave a worthy portion; for he loved Hannah."

Earthly kings and princes are called the children of the most High, and God gives 'em, all of them, portions. Their portion is their worldly kingdoms, and the pleasure, wealth and glory thereto belonging. But they ben't the firstborn, but the saints, and therefore they have a more worthy portion than they. God gives them something far better than earthly crowns, and all the glory of earthly kingdoms.

And as of old the firstborn sons used to be the priests of the house. So the saints are the priests of the world, the house which God hath built, and their work is to offer up spiritual sacrifices

---

2. JE cites vv. 5–6.

unto God. I Pet. 2:5, "Ye also, as lively stones, are built up a spiritual house, an holy priesthood, to offer up spiritual sacrifices, acceptable to God by Jesus Christ"; and Is. 61:5–6, "And strangers shall stand and feed your flocks, and the sons of the alien shall be your plowmen and your vinedressers. But ye shall be named the priests of the Lord: men shall call you the ministers of our God: ye shall eat the riches of the gentiles, and in their glory shall ye boast yourselves."

In the days of the patriarchs, he that had the birthright inherited the blessing of Abraham, consisting in the promise of Canaan, and the promise of Christ, in whom all the families of the earth should be blessed. So the saints in this sense have the privileges of the birthright, in that the blessing of Abraham comes on them. As Gal. 3:14, "That the blessing of Abraham might come on the gentiles through Jesus Christ; that we might receive the promise of the Spirit through faith."

They are the heirs of the heavenly crown, and theirs is the promised seed, Jesus Christ, and all those blessings that come by him.

And as the firstborn sons of kings of old were wont to inherit the kingdom, so the saints in this sense have the right of the firstborn children of God, in that they are heirs of his kingdom. Jas. 2:5, "Hath not [God] chosen the poor of this world rich in faith, heirs of the kingdom which the Lord hath promised to them that love him?"

As they inherit the priesthood, and are priests unto God, so they also inherit the kingdom, and are kings. Rev. 5:10, "[Thou] hath made us kings and priests unto our God: and we shall reign on the earth."

(2) The saints, in some respects, have peculiar privileges above the angels. The angels are called the sons of God, but we nowhere find them called God's firstborn, though they are creatures of so much more extensive faculties, and nobler natures, than men. But the saints are several times called God's firstborn, as not only in the text, but in Ex. 4:22–23, "And thou shalt say unto Pharaoh, Thus saith the Lord, Israel is my son, even my firstborn: and I say

unto thee, Let my son go, that he may serve me: and if thou refuse to let him [go, behold,] I will slay thy son, even thy firstborn."

This imports that God intends, in some respects at least, to set this child higher than other children, and to bestow upon it greater privileges. As 'tis said of Christ in the 89th Psalm,[3] [v. 27], "I will make him my firstborn, higher than the kings of the earth," so the church, God's Israel, is in the love and favor of God set higher in some respects, set higher than other children. As God hath made Christ his firstborn, by setting him higher both than earthly princes, and also than heavenly thrones and principalities; so his saints, his spouse, his members, in some respect partake with him in this privilege. God has, for his sake, made them his firstborn. And 'tis a further argument that 'tis not only with respect to other men that the saints are called God's firstborn, but also with respect to the angels, because in the text, when the church of saints is mentioned together with the company of angels, they are called the firstborn. First 'tis said, "to an innumerable company of angels," and then, in the next words, "to the general assembly and church of the firstborn." Which seems to intimate as if the general assembly of the church of saints, was to be looked upon as having the birthright above the company of angels, as they doubtless have in some respects.

Christ never put such honor on the angels as he has on the saints. He has not taken their nature upon him, but he now reigns in heaven, and will reign to all eternity, in men's nature, over angels and over all things. The saints have a greater interest, and a closer union with Christ, than the angels: for they are said to be his spouse, and members of his body, of his flesh and of his bones. Christ has never given so wonderful a manifestation of his love to the angels, as he has to the saints: for he has died for the saints, but he never did so for the angels. The angels were created to be subservient to Christ in the work of men's redemption, and to be ministering spirits to the saints. Christ's peculiar delights are with elect men; Prov. 8:30, "rejoicing in the habitable parts of his earth; and my delights were with the sons of men." And the angels are

---

3. JE cites Ps. 87.

said to be "their angels" [Matt. 18:10], but with respect [to] the angels, the saints are nowhere said to [be] their saints.

Having thus shown why the church of Christ is called the church of the firstborn, I come now, in the

Third place, to show how their names are written in heaven. They are so, two ways:

1. As they were from all eternity written in the book of God's decrees among the elect. Thus we read of their names being written in the book of life from the foundation of the world. Rev. 13:8, "And all that dwell upon the earth shall worship him, whose names are not written in the book of life of the Lamb slain from the foundation of the world." Their names may on this account be said to be written in heaven, as God, whose decree it is, is said to dwell in heaven, and as by this decree they are appointed to dwell in heaven.

2. Their names are written in heaven, as they are enrolled among the saints, the citizens of heaven. It has been the custom in many great cities, to keep records of the names of the citizens, or those that had a right to the privileges of the city. So it was at Rome, and so it seems to have [been] at Jerusalem. The Jews' records of the names of the Jews that had any part in Jerusalem, or any right to come and worship there, were written in the rolls of that city; and so they were said to have a "memorial in Jerusalem." Therefore Nehemiah tells Tobiah and Sanballat, Neh. 2:20, that they had no memorial in Jerusalem; i.e., their names were not written in the rolls of that city.

So as soon as a man is truly converted, he is accepted as a saint or a citizen of heaven, as one that has a part and inheritance there; and accordingly his name is as it were enrolled in the rolls of that glorious city.

APPLICATION.

Use I [is] of *Instruction*.

First. These things do further show the great honor and blessedness that the saints are admitted to, who are come to the general {assembly and church of the firstborn, which are written in heaven}. How great a privilege [it] is for us, who are naturally so far off, to be assembled together to Christ, and united to so glorious a head, and in him, one to another; and to belong to that assembly, who have their place of assembly in heaven, and be of those that are actually on their way thither.

How great a privilege it is, not only to be some of the children of God, but also to be ranked among those that are called his firstborn, to have those peculiar privileges that belong to such; to have a more precious and worthy portion that is appropriated to the firstborn, while others have their portion in worldly good things, and are sent away from God; to be some of those that are kept at home, to dwell with God as his heirs; to have a so much more excellent portion than earthly kings, that are, all of them, said to be the children of the most High; to be as the firstborn of God, kings and priests unto him; to be in some respects privileged even above the angels themselves, who are nowhere called God's firstborn; to be [the] spouse and members of Christ, who is the firstborn of every creature, to be as the objects of his dying love, and his special delight: and as such, to have our names written in heaven, to have our names enrolled in the records of that glorious city as some of the citizens, and so to have good evidence that our names were eternally written in the Lamb's book of life. This is greater cause of rejoicing to any, than the enjoyment of all earthly good things, or the greatest temporal privileges that can be conceived of; yea, much greater than to have a spirit of prophecy, or power to work miracles. As is evident by Luke 10:20, "Nevertheless in this rejoice not, [that the spirits are subject unto you; but rather rejoice, because your names are written in heaven]."

Second. This may also lead us to a sense of the misery of all unregenerate persons, who are so far from being the subjects of these privileges; who have their portions in the mean things of this world; are sent away from God with them, as it were into a state of banishment; are cast out, as the son of the bondwoman was, that they mayn't be suffered to be heirs with the sons of the free woman [Gen. 21:10]; who have no memorial in Jerusalem; whose names are not written amongst the living there, but are written in the earth with the dead, as some of those that are dead in trespasses and sins; who don't belong to the general assembly and church of the firstborn, but are of the synagogue of Satan, and are hasting to that great congregation, or mixed multitude and throng, made up of devils and wicked men that are in hell; who if they continue as they are, will in a little while be of the congregation of the dead, and then shall have their souls gathered with sinners, and will at the day of judgment appear with [the] hasting crew that shall stand at Christ's left hand, and shall receive the accursed sentence from him.

Use II [is of] *Exhortation.*
First. Let us who visibly belong to the general assembly {and church of the firstborn}, be exhorted diligently and devoutly to attend the public assemblies of God's people in this world. The public, worshipping assemblies of God's people in this world, are appointed of God to subserve to the designs of that universal assembling of all the saints unto Christ, and their assembling together in heaven hereafter, and is some image of it. By such a solemn assembling of Christians in this world, the nature of the gospel church, as it is a multitude of persons assembled unto Christ, is represented and made visible.

They therefore that despise such assemblies, and either neglect them or allow themselves in an irreverent, or a very careless and formal, negligent way of attending on them, discover sad marks of their having never yet truly come to the general assembly and {church of the firstborn}. And it looks darkly upon them, as though they were [not] in the way to the place of their assembly, even heaven. All that are of that general assembly are God's sincere worshippers, who delight in his worship, who love the habitation of God's house, and "in whose hearts are the ways of them"; who "go from strength to strength," that love and long to "appear before God" [Ps. 26:8; 84:5–7; 42:2].

Sermon 4

Therefore as you either profess now, or hope hereafter, to be of that blessed assembly, don't allow yourself in a lifeless, sleepy way of attending {public worship}, but attend with the utmost diligence and reverence, as setting yourself in the presence of God, and considering the house of God as the gate of heaven [Gen. 28:17].

Second. Seeing you visibly belong to the church of the firstborn, take heed that you don't sell your birthright for a morsel of meat, as Esau did. The apostle Paul gives this caution, in the context of those words that we have been insisting on this day, 15th, 16th[, and] 17th verses of the chapter: "Looking diligently lest any man fail of the grace of God; lest any root of bitterness springing up trouble you, and thereby many be defiled; lest there be any fornicator, or profane person, as Esau, who for one morsel of meat sold his birthright. For ye know how that afterward, when he would have inherited the blessing, he was rejected: for he found no place of repentance, though he sought it carefully with tears."

How great was Esau's folly, to sell so great privileges as belonged to him as Isaac's firstborn, such as the honor of the priesthood, and the inheritance of the blessing of Abraham, which respected not only his own lifetime but future generations: I say, how great was his folly in selling such great privileges, for so small a matter as just the present gratifying of his appetite with a mess of pottage when he was hungry. How light did he make of those privileges, to part with them at such a rate. How well might the Holy Ghost set such a mark on his contempt of them, in relating the story, as in Gen. 25:34, "Then Jacob gave Esau bread and pottage of lentils; and he did eat and drink, and rose up, and went his way: thus Esau despised his birthright."

Don't follow an example of such great folly and profaneness. Don't sell the privileges that belong to the church of the firstborn for a moment's pleasure, when[4] you are solicited by some eager, sensual appetite, or for a little worldly gain, which may well be compared to a morsel of meat. Don't do that which is contrary to the commands of God, for such a trifle. Consider the consequences

---

4. At this point in the MS, LL. 11–12, JE incorporated a portion of a discarded letter (no. 24, printed in WJE 16:81–82).

of Esau's folly: his short, momentary pleasure with his mess of pottage, cost him long sorrow and repentance, bitter crying and tears, and all to no purpose. Don't gratify your lusts for the present, trusting to a repentance hereafter. Mind what the Apostle says concerning Esau, to deter you from this folly: "For ye know how that afterward, when he would have inherited the blessing, he was rejected: for he found no place of repentance, though he sought it carefully with tears." And Esau is not the only instance of this kind. There are doubtless many thousands that have tasted of forbidden fruit against the light of their own consciences, and so have in effect sold their birthright, and the blessing belonging to it, trusting to future repentance.

SERMON 5

How Christians Are Come to God the Judge of All

Hebrews 12:22–24.

And to God the Judge of all.

We are come now to the

V. [Fifth] particular in the text, to show how Christians are come to God the Judge of all.

And in order to this, I would,

First. Show who the person is here spoken of.

Second. How he, in a peculiar manner, is said to be the Judge of all.

Third. How Christians are said to be come to this Judge of all.

First. It may be inquired who this is, that is here spoken of. The words themselves show that 'tis God that is spoken of, but that don't fully resolve the question: for there are more persons than one that are God. God the Father, and Jesus Christ, and the Holy Ghost, are each of them called God in Scripture.

And sometimes when God is spoken of, no one particular person in the Godhead is intended more than another, but what is intended is the deity or the divine nature common to all the persons in the Trinity, and all the persons are included. But when God is spoken of in this place, 'tis not the deity or the divine essence, as common to all the persons, that seems to be intended. All the persons of the Trinity are not included.

But the answer to the inquiry is that:

God the Father is the person spoken of, and is here said to be the Judge of all. 'Tis not the Son, nor the Holy Ghost, nor the deity as including all the persons, but the Father particularly: and this is manifest by the distinction that is made in the text between God the Judge, and Jesus the mediator. Here Christians are said to be come "to God the Judge of all"; and in the next clause but one, they are said to be come to Jesus the mediator of the new covenant, which makes it manifest that they are two distinct persons that are spoken of. And the manifest distinction and the mutual relation of the two offices, makes it manifest that they are two distinct persons that are spoken [of]: one of them having the office or doing the part of judge; and the other acting as mediator before that judge. Which shows the person that is called "the Judge of all" to be God the Father, for he is the Judge before whom Christ appears as mediator. He is the lawgiver and Judge that required satisfaction to be made to the law, that expects a righteousness that shall answer the law; and he is the Judge to whom this satisfaction and righteousness is presented, and who accepts of it; and he is the person that acquits and justifies the sinner on account of Christ's satisfaction and righteousness: for 'tis the part of a judge to accept a satisfaction to a law, and 'tis the part of a judge to justify a person as having answered that law, and being righteous according to the law.

But this matter may be more fully explained under the next head, viz., the

Second thing that was proposed, which is to show how God the Father, in a particular manner, is said to be the Judge of all as distinguished from the other persons of the Trinity.

In order the more fully to understand this, the following things may be noted:

Sermon 5

1. Among the three persons of the Trinity, each one has as it were his distinct place or office assigned him, by agreement among themselves. There is that which the Scripture, speaking of God after the manner of men, represents as a consultation and agreement among the persons of the Trinity, respecting the divine acts and disposals towards men, assigning to each one his part or distinct office in the management or transactions of divine providence towards them. Thus in Zech. 6:13, "the counsel of peace" is said to be between the Father and the Son. This disposition of things among the persons of the Trinity, whereby each one has his distinct office, is what divines commonly call the œconomy of the persons of the Trinity.

2. By this agreement, the place or office of God the Father is to be the giver, the defender[,] and judge of the law. God the Father, by the just agreement or covenant of all the persons, is the person that is to maintain the rights of the Godhead; that is to be his personal office, to maintain the authority and majesty of the deity. And therefore it belongs to him especially to be the lawgiver, and to defend the divine law, to see to it that the authority of the law be defended. And so 'tis his peculiar office not only to give the law, but, as he has the care of its defense, he is the judge. He is the person that is to have the care of avenging rebellion against the law, and the dishonor done to it. And it belongs to him to judge when the law is answered, or satisfied, and to accept the satisfaction.

And therefore, when Christ as mediator undertook to make satisfaction to the law, he made the satisfaction to the Father. The Father was the person to whom it belonged to require this satisfaction, and to accept it, because he was the person whose office it was to be the defender and judge of the law. Otherwise, it would have been no more proper that the satisfaction should be offered to God the Father, than to God the Son or the Holy Ghost.

As the office of the Father was to be the giver, defender[,] and judge of the law, so the office that the Son was appointed to, was to be the mediator between God and the sinners that had violated the law. He, by appointment, was to be a person that in his office was to act under the Father, as being appointed by him and interceding before him, or paying a price to him and seeking acceptance of him.

The office of the Holy Ghost was to be the emissary or messenger of the other persons. He, in his office, is to act under both the others, to execute that which way is made by the other two in their office, to accomplish the success of the negotiations that are between the Father and the Son.

These several distinct parts and offices that here are undertaken by each person of the Trinity, are maintained according to that covenant which they have entered into from eternity. And by this covenant, 'tis peculiarly the place of the Father to be "Judge of all."

It is as Judge that the mediator appears before him. It was as judge of the law that God the Father required satisfaction, and it was as Judge that he accepted the satisfaction that Christ made. It was as Judge that he justified Christ, and acquitted and rewarded him after he had made full satisfaction of the law for sin. And it is as judge of the law that God the Father acquits and justifies sinners that believe in Christ. Redemption belongs to the Son, but justification peculiarly belongs to the office of God the Father. Christ works out a righteousness for sinners, but 'tis God the Father that justifies 'em for that righteousness. But justifying and condemning are judicial acts, or the acts of a judge.

And therefore,

3. It may be objected that God is the Judge of all, in a manner that neither of the other of the persons of the Trinity are. The other persons in the Trinity, in some sense, may be said to judge men. The Holy Ghost doth so, as he awakens and convinces men "of sin, of righteousness and of judgment" [John 16:8], and brings 'em to judge and condemn them; but in this he only acts under the Father, by setting home the Father's law upon them, and convincing them of his righteous judgments.

But the greatest difficulty is with respect to God the Son: how being Judge of all should be the peculiar office of the Father, when Jesus Christ, or God the Son, is often said in Scripture to be appointed to be judge of the world. And we are often told that he is the person that shall appear at the last day to judge the world. Yea, this business of judging seems to be ascribed to the Son, rather than the Father, in John 5:22, "The Father judgeth no man, but [hath committed all judgment unto the Son]."

But what the Scripture says of Christ's being appointed judge of the world, is indeed no objection against what has been laid down. There is really [no] difficulty in reconciling this with the Father's being called Judge of all, and his being so in a peculiar manner, and that being his proper office by the agreement of the persons of the Trinity among themselves: for he is nevertheless the Judge of all in a manner that the Son is not. Which will plainly appear by two things:

(1) God the Father acts the part of a judge towards Jesus Christ, Christ himself, as mediator. Christ, though merely as a divine person, and considered as prior to any voluntary agreement among the persons of the Trinity, is equal to the Father, and not properly subject to him; yet in his office of mediator, which he has voluntarily undertaken, is subject to God the Father. And therefore Christ says, as in the 14th [chapter] of John, [v.] 28, "My Father is greater than I." "[My Father which gave them me is] greater than all," John 10:29. In this office, God the Father was Christ's lawgiver. When he sent him into the world, he gave him a law that he was to obey; and as he was his lawgiver, so also he was his judge. And Christ acted towards him as his judge, and he committed himself to him as his judge. And therefore the Apostle, speaking of Christ, says he "committed himself to him that judgeth righteously," I Pet. 2:23.

God the Father was Christ's judge, to whom it belonged to judge whether he had obeyed his law or no, and he did judge him. And after he had done the work that the Father had appointed him, he acquitted him as his judge; he justified him. I Tim. 3:16, "God [was] manifest in the flesh, justified in the Spirit."

As his judge he raised him from the dead, and as his judge he exalted him to his own right hand in heaven, and rewarded him for his well doing.

(2) Christ is the judge of the world only by delegation from the Father, and as the Father's representative. Judgment originally belongs to God the Father; 'tis his proper office to judge all. But yet that don't hinder but that the Father may appoint another judge under him, to act in his name. He "hath committed judgment to the Son" [John 5:22]. Christ, as God-man and mediator, is the Judge of the world in the same way as he is Lord of the world. He is Lord or King of the world, as God-man and mediator, no otherwise than by a delegated and representative authority. The Father hath committed to him the government of the world; he hath exalted him, and set him upon his throne, and said, "Let all the angels of God worship him" [Heb. 1:6]. He hath put all things under his feet, and he governs the world in his mediatorial kingdom and as head over all things to the church, by virtue of authority received from the Father, who hath set this his king on his "holy hill of Zion," Ps. 2:6. And therefore, when the designs of his mediatorial kingdom shall be fully accomplished, he shall resign up the kingdom again to the Father, of[1] whom he received it, and to whom it originally belongs. I Cor. 15:24, "Then cometh the end, when he shall have delivered up the kingdom to God, even the Father; when he shall have put down all rule and all authority and power." [V.] 28, "And when all things shall be subdued unto him, then shall the Son also himself be subject unto him that put all things under him, that God may be all in all."

And so it is that he is the Judge of the world. 'Tis by powers received from the Father. John 5:27, the Father "hath given him authority to execute judgment also, because he is the Son of man."

And therefore, when he comes into the world at the last day, he will come in the Father's name and in his Father's glory. Matt. 16:27,[2] "For the Son of man shall come in the glory of his Father with his angels; and then shall he reward every man according to his works."

Christ is the judge of the world, in the same manner as he is the lawgiver. The Son of God was improved by the Father, in his

1. MS: "to."
2. MS: John 16:27.

Sermon 5

name, to give laws to men. It was he, most immediately, that gave the law at Mt. Sinai; as appears by Acts 7:38, "This is he, that was in the church in the wilderness with the angel which spoke to him in the Mt. Sinai and with our fathers: who received the lively oracles to give unto us." God the Father is never called an angel.

But Christ gave the law as the Father's representative, and so he is the judge of the law.

I come now, in the

Third place, to show how Christians are said to be come to God the Father as Judge of all. And in order to a right understanding of this, it must be first noted, in the general, that the Apostle here doubtless has respect to something that is a distinguishing privilege that Christians have by the gospel, or covenant of grace.

The context makes this plain: for all these things, from the beginning to the end, are distinguishing privileges that Christians[3] have by the gospel. Christians are not come, the Apostle says, to Mt. Sinai, but they are come to Mt. Sion, "the city of the living God," etc.; i.e., the gospel brings them to privileges that they could not be brought to by the law that was given at Mt. Sinai. What they are brought to at Mt. Sion, are the privileges they are brought to by the gospel, as distinguished from the law that was given at Mt. Sinai in so terrible a manner.

Now therefore, the question is, How the Apostle mentions coming to God the Judge of all as a distinguishing gospel privilege that Christians are brought to at Mt. Sion, above what the children of Israel were brought to at Mt. Sinai.

At Mt. Sinai, the children of Israel stood before God as a strict lawgiver and judge. God sat at Mt. Sinai on the throne of strict justice, and those that never received or heard the gospel, yet they shall be brought to appear before God the Judge of all, as well others; everyone must stand before his judgment seat.

And therefore, how is a coming to God the Judge of all here to [be] mentioned as the peculiar privilege of Christians, that

---

3. MS: "X."

they obtain by the gospel or covenant of grace, and that they are brought to at Mt. Sion?

Here, the consideration of three things will clear up this difficulty:

1. 'Tis to be considered that God, in his proceedings with believers by the gospel or covenant of grace, don't in the least divest himself of the character of a strict judge. Indeed, there are some things that he does in the character of a sovereign, but nothing to the prejudice of his other character as a strict judge, and as judge of the law. He appears under the gospel, not only as sitting on a throne of strict justice, but also as sitting on a throne of sovereign grace; but he don't sit on a throne of grace in such a manner as at all to remove from the throne of justice. He acts as sitting on both those thrones in the gracious promises of the gospel, and in the bestowment of the blessed privileges of it.

In giving Christ to fulfill the law for us, and in making a new covenant with men, God acts as a sovereign; but these acts of sovereignty don't at all prejudice his character as a strict judge of the law, because he does something herein that the law did not direct to. Yet he does nothing contrary to the law in it. But after Christ is given and has fulfilled the law, God, in bestowing the blessings that Christ has purchased, still acts as a strict judge of the law. He, in justifying and rewarding believers in Christ, does as much do the part of a strict judge of the law as in eternally condemning sinners. Rom. 3:25–26, "Whom God hath set forth to be a propitiation through faith in his blood, to declare his righteousness for the remission of sins that are past, through the forbearance of God; to declare, I say, at this time his righteousness: that he might be just, and the justifier of him that believes in Jesus."

God, in all that he has done for his people in the way of the covenant of grace, never has receded from the throne of his justice, and never will, and does as much sit on the throne of justice on Mt. Sion as he did at Mt. Sinai; though he don't there sit only on a throne of justice as he did at Mt. Sinai, but also on a throne of grace.

2. 'Tis the great privilege that Christians have by the gospel, that though God still acts as a strict judge, yet they are brought to acceptance and favor and strict union with this judge. Though God don't at all divest himself of the character of a strict judge of the law, yet so is the matter wisely and wonderfully ordered through Christ, that those that have sinned and broken the law are brought to this great God, so as to [be] accepted of him, and received into favor and the most intimate union with him, and full enjoyment of him acting as a strict judge. Thus 'tis the peculiar privilege that Christians have by the gospel, to come to God the judge.

Others that are under the law, can't come and have access to the strict Judge of all after this manner: for God is a consuming fire to them that are under the law. This is a privilege that persons are brought to nowhere else but at Mt. Sion. The children of Israel could not come nigh to this strict judge at Mt. Sinai; for as the Apostle observes in the 20th verse of the context, "if so much as a beast touch the mountain, he must be stoned, or thrust through with a dart."

3. Though Christians come to God as a judge, yet 'tis their peculiar privilege not to come to him as a lawgiver, in the manner men did under the first covenant. Christians, or believers in Christ, appear before God as a judge as much as ever, and God acts as a judge of the law in justifying and rewarding them for the righteousness of Christ. So they are brought before God as a judge as much as unbelievers that have no interest in the covenant of grace. But they don't appear before God as a lawgiver in the same sense that men did under the first covenant: for then, God gave man the law for him to fulfill, and at Mt. Sinai the law was given to men that are under the law, as exacting it of them to fulfill it themselves, upon pain of damnation. But the law is not thus given to Christians at Mt. Sion, as exacting a fulfillment of them, because Christ has already fulfilled it for them. Christ has already appeared before God as a lawgiver for them, and they now only come to him as a judge to receive the reward of his obedience.

APPLICATION.

Here is matter of great consolation to true Christians, and terror and conviction to others.

I. Here is just ground of great consolation and rejoicing to true Christians.

What has been said, shows the sure grounds that Christians' hopes of happiness are built upon. There is every way ground for strong consolation unto them. There is great consolation that they may fetch from the throne of grace that God sits on in Mt. Sion; and not only [so], but there is also strong consolation to be derived from the throne of justice that God also sits upon there. Not only the infinite mercy of God, but also the strict, immovable and immutable justice of God is for them. Both law and gospel with united voice call for their happiness and eternal glory.

The foundation of their blessedness can no more be shaken, than God's throne can be shaken. Yea, both his thrones, his throne of grace and his throne of judgment, may as soon be overthrown as their blessedness can be overthrown. We may be sure that God's throne is settled fast on a strong foundation. It is said that 'tis "established of old"; Ps. 93:2, "Thy throne is established of old."

And the Christian's blessedness is settled on a foundation equally strong and immovable.

If God had only revealed that his mercy was infinite and sufficient to bestow blessedness on the saints, and had promised it on that ground, that would have been sure ground of hope; but that the heirs of promise may have more strong consolation and firm hope, not only God's mercy and truth, but his justice as a strict judge are revealed to be on their side.

It may well remove all their doubts and fears, to consider that they are not come to Mt. Sinai to receive the law as enjoined upon them, and a perfect observance of it exacted of them, because Christ has been to Mt. Sinai for them, and has received the law and has fulfilled it; and all that remains for them is only to come to God at Mt. Sion as a judge, and to be acquitted and justified and rewarded by him as such for the obedience that is already wrought out.

It may justly be matter of great rejoicing to you, that though God be so strict a judge, yet there is way made that you may have access to him, may be accepted of him, and may be blessed in him forever: and that, though you have so greatly sinned against him.

It may be matter of rejoicing to you, that God does sit on a throne of strict justice as he does, and that he is so holy and righteous a judge. For your happiness is so much the more sure for it.

II. What has been said, may justly suggest matter of terrors to all that are not true Christians. For when you hear that Christians are come to God the Judge of all, you have it to consider of,

That 'tis impossible you should have any friendly access to or favor with this great and strict judge, in the state that you are in. God will be a consuming fire to all such as you in his throne of judgment; he will burn up all that come nigh, with fire unquenchable. Thus he appeared as a consuming fire at Mt. Sinai: the mount was altogether in a smoke; there was a terrible fire, Deut. 4:36, Deut. 5:5 and 18:16; and it burnt in such a terrible manner, that the flames ascended up, as 'tis said, "even to the midst of heaven," Deut. 4:11. How can you come to God in Mt. Sinai, which [is] all round encompassed with fierce lightnings, and has bounds set about, which if any man broke through, the Lord would brake forth upon him and consume; yea, if so much as "a beast touch the mount he shall be stoned, or thrust through with a dart"? How much more shall a guilty, provoking rebel be thrust through with the darts of divine vengeance?

And you are [to] consider, that though you can't have acceptance with such a Judge, yet you must have to do with him; you can't get out of his hands; you must stand before this great Judge: and how dreadful will his holiness and justice and almighty power be to you then? Can your hands be strong, or "abide the day of his coming? Who shall stand when he appears? He will be as a refiner's fire, and fullers' soap" [Mal. 3:2]. "The day of the Lord shall burn as an oven, and all the wicked of the earth shall be as stubble" [Mal. 4:1].

You little conceive how dreadful a thing it will be to stand before such a Judge in your sins, and with the guilt of all the sins that ever you have committed. You little conceive how dismal astonishment, and those heart shrinkings and horrible amazement will be, that will then seize upon you. O! how ready will you be [to] hide "in the caves and dens of the earth" [Heb. 11:38]. But how will all be in vain, when you must stand before his judgment seat, and must receive the awful sentence out [of] his mouth, and must bear the eternal execution of it.

III. This may be matter of conviction to sinners of their necessity of a mediator, in order to their access to God. If God not only sat on Sinai, but also sits on Mt. Sion as a strict judge, as on a throne of strict justice, then doubtless we can never have access to him but through one that has fulfilled and satisfied the law. And 'tis in vain for you to hope to have access or acceptance by your own righteousness.

If God only sat on a throne of grace, and not on a throne of justice; if he had receded from his law and had divested himself of the character of a strict judge for sinners' sakes, there might be some hope that you might be accepted without a perfect righteousness. But this he never has done, and never will do, and heaven and earth shall pass away sooner than "one jot or one tittle shall pass from the law" [Matt. 5:18]. Therefore you may well eternally despair of ever coming to God, so as to have union and favor with him in any way but by Jesus Christ.

SERMON 6

How Christians Are Come to the Spirits of Just Men Made Perfect

Hebrews 12:22–24.

And to the spirits of just men made perfect.

This is the

[VI.] *Sixth* particular mentioned in the text. And that I may the more clearly show how Christians are come to the spirits of just men made perfect, I would,

First. Speak something of the spirits of just men made perfect; and,

Second. Show [how] Christians are said to be come to those spirits.

[*First.*] In speaking of the spirits of just men made perfect, I would,

1. Show what are meant by these spirits of just men made perfect;

2. [Show] in what respects they are the spirits of just men; and,

3. [Show] how they are made perfect.

[*First*. Speak something of the spirits of just men made perfect.]

1. The *First Inquiry* may be, What spirits are intended by these "spirits of just men made perfect."

Answer. The departed spirits of saints, or the souls of those saints that are dead. For though sincerely good men are often in Scripture language said to be perfect men, even while they live here in this world, yet 'tis very manifest that the spirits that are spoken of here, are not the souls of good men in the present state, but in their state of separation from the body. If all that had been intended by this expression, had been only that Christians were come to be of the family of good men upon earth, 'tis not likely that the Apostle would have said, "the spirits of just men," as though the body was purposely excluded in the expression. 'Tis not agreeable to the language of Scripture, when speaking of the church of good men in this world, to say the spirits of saints, or spirits of just men: but while they dwell in the body, they are called "the saints," "the faithful in Christ Jesus" and the like, without distinguishing their spirits.

But this manner of speech is agreeable to the language of the Scripture, when speaking of the souls of the dead. Thus the apostle Peter, [when speaking] of the souls of wicked men that are dead, calls 'em "the spirits in prison," I Pet. 3:19.[1]

And that the Apostle here is speaking of the departed souls of saints in heaven, is further confirmed from that, that the spirits of just men made perfect are mentioned among other things that are in heaven, as with the "innumerable company of angels," and with "God the Judge of all," and "Jesus the mediator of the new covenant," which have their dwelling place in heaven.

And so far as any place is intended, heaven is intended by these expressions of Mt. Sion, "the city of the living God," "the heavenly Jerusalem," and "the general assembly and church of the firstborn." Though they are not all in heaven, yet they are said to be written in heaven. The

---

1. MS: "II Pet. 3:19."

Sermon 6

2. [*Second*] *Inquiry* is, in what respects these are the spirits of just men, or in what respects they were just men, whose spirits they were.

Answ[er]. They were so in two respects: by an imputed righteousness, and by inherent holiness.

(1) The saints are called just men, by the righteousness of Christ imputed to them. No man is just or righteous in the eye of the law, but he that is perfectly so; and therefore the Wise Man says, Eccles. 7:20, "There is not a just man upon earth, that doth good, and sinneth not." In that as there is not a "man upon earth that doth good, and sinneth not," therefore there is not a just man upon earth, that is just in his own righteousness, in the eye of the law.

So no man is just in the sight of God by his own justice. And therefore Job says, Job 9:2, "How should man be just with God?"

And yet believers are justified, or accepted as just with God, yea, and just in the eye of the law, though it be said, 143rd Psalm, 2nd verse, that in his sight, no flesh living should be justified. To be justified, according to the literal construction of the word, is to be made just. Believers are just, strictly so, by the imputation of a righteousness that perfectly answers the most exact rule of justice. As that justice or righteousness is properly theirs by a real interest and propriety they have in it, so they by it do truly become just or righteous men.

(2) The saints, in another sense, are called just men by reason of their inherent holiness. They have no legal righteousness inherent in them, yet they have true holiness, which is often called justice and righteousness in Scripture. They are holy in heart. They have all holy principles and dispositions. They truly love righteousness, and hate all wickedness. They are sincere and upright in heart, and hate every evil and false way. And they are just in their conversations. They are righteous in their behavior towards God and towards men. They conform to that rule in Mic. 6:8, "He hath showed thee, O man, what is good; and what doth the Lord require of thee, but to do justly, and to love mercy, and to walk humbly with thy God"; and to that, Tit. 2:12, "Teaching us that denying all

ungodliness and worldly lusts, we should live soberly, righteously, and godly, in this present world."

'Tis their earnest endeavors, as it was the Apostle's, to keep consciences "void of offense towards God and towards men" [Acts 24:16]. "And whatsoever things are true, whatsoever are honest, whatsoever things are just," they think on those things, Philip. 4:8.

And though in this world they don't actually perform a righteousness that answers the perfect rule of righteousness that God has given men, his holy and strict law, yet in heart they are so far conformed to that law, that they delight in it after the inner man [Rom. 7:22]. They love it for its holiness, strictness and perfection. The law of God is not at all too strict for them: they would not love the better if it were less strict, but the less. Ps. 119:140, "Thy word is very pure: therefore thy servant loveth it."

And 'tis their fervent desire to be perfectly conformed to this strict law, in heart and life, and 'tis their constant aim and endeavor so to be. They make the law their rule. Though they, through infirmity of the flesh, fail of coming up to it, yet the perfection which this rule requires, is the pole star by which they steer, and the mark they continually aim at.

Thus those men whose spirits—the departed spirits in heaven—were just men.

I come now,

3. [*Third,*] to *Inquire* how these spirits in heaven are made perfect. They may be said to be made perfect in two respects: with respect to their past state of probation that is finished, and their state of glory which they are now arrived at.

(1) They may be said to be made perfect with respect [to] their past state of probation in that now, all that pertained to their state of probation and preparation for glory, is finished. That in Scripture language is said to be perfected that is finished. So those that are dead, are sometimes said to be perfected in this sense, that is, all that concerns them in this life is finished; all that God intended, by placing them here in this world, is completed. This is doubtless partly intended by Christ when he, speaking of his own

Sermon 6

death, says, as in Luke 13:32, "Behold I cast out devils, and I do cures today and tomorrow, and the third day I shall be perfected"; i.e., "the third day" (meaning the third year) "I shall die. My life here shall be finished, and all that concerns me in my present state, shall have an end." Christ don't mean, "The third day I shall be made perfect in holiness": for he was perfect in holiness already, and never was otherwise.

So the saints, when dead, are said to be perfected, or made perfect, as the work which God intended 'em in their state of preparation for glory is ended. They have finished their course, which God intended they should run. They have finished their warfare, they have obtained a complete victory, and all God's providential dispensations towards them, which he intended as preparatives to their everlasting state, are finished. There were many things they had to do, and many things that were to be done with them in providence, in order to their being vessels of mercy, prepared to glory; but now all those things are finished completely, and in this respect, they are as full, ripe fruit gathered into the garner of God. Of old, the stones of the temple were all hewed and exactly fitted for their place in the temple, before they were brought there, so that there was no noise of hammer or ax in building that noble structure [I Kgs. 6:7]. So the end of all God's dealings with the saints, all the means of grace they enjoy and all God's providences towards them in this present state, is to fit them for their heavenly temple. But when life is ended, the hewing is done; then the squaring of the stone, as with hammer and ax, is completed. The end that God aimed at in these things, then is obtained. Things concerning them have an end, as Christ said of himself. Luke 22:37, "For I say unto you, that this that is written must yet be accomplished in me, And he was reckoned among the transgressors: for the things concerning me have an end."

(2) The departed spirits of saints may be said to be made perfect, with respect to the state that they are arrived at.

1. The departed spirits of the saints are arrived at their rest and their end. That may be said to be in its perfect state, that comes to that state that its nature craves and tends to. Thus men, while in

a state of childhood, are said not to be perfect men, because nature has still another state in view that it tends and approaches [to]. But when men are grown up, then they are said to come to that perfect stature, and to the state of perfect men. Then nature rests, and don't seek anything further in that kind.

So the saints, in their present state in this world, are not in a state of rest: the new nature han't obtained its end. Its canton is as it were still at a distance. The saints here are out of their proper place, at a distance from their portion. But in heaven, they are come to their rest, have obtained their end; they then are come to their fixed and everlasting state, have obtained their inheritance and are come to their place where they are to be forever.

2. They are made perfect in the state they are arrived at, with respect to the excellency and glory of that state. But here, for the more distinct and clear understanding of this, it must be noted:

a. That the glory of the departed souls of saints, is not in its highest and ultimate perfection. This is reserved for the resurrection, when their spirits shall be united with their bodies again, and shall be glorified together with ['em]. As the highest punishment of the devils and damned souls is reserved for the day of judgment, so the greatest reward of the saints is reserved till that time. And therefore, that day is always spoken of in the New Testament as the day wherein the saints shall especially receive their reward, and enter into the joy of their Lord. But yet,

b. The glory of the departed souls of saints, may truly in several respects be said to be perfect, and particularly in these two respects:

(a) 'Tis perfect with a relative or comparative perfection, i.e., as compared with their state here in this world. When compared with the present state, it is a state of manhood, wherein the saints are arrived at the stature of men. The saints in the present state, are represented as in a state of childhood, in comparison of what they will be hereafter. So it is in I Cor. 13[:10–11], "[But when that which is perfect is come, then that which is in part shall be done away. When I was a child, I spake as a child, I understood as a

Sermon 6

child, I thought as a child: but when I became a man, I put away childish things]."

The present state is an exceeding imperfect state. The knowledge, and holiness and joy of the separated souls of the saints in heaven, shall exceedingly transcend all that the most eminent saints arrive at here.

What they obtain here is but as the morning twilight, but the state of the saints in heaven is perfect day, such as is by the immediate rays of the sun.

Not only the degree of excellency and blessedness that they shall be the subjects of, will be immensely greater, but also the means and manner of their knowing God, and serving and enjoying him, will be inconceivably more excellent and perfect. They shall see God more immediately, not through a glass as they do here, but face to face, and shall converse with him more immediately [I Cor. 13:12].

(b) The perfection of their glory is absolute, with respect to the removal of opposite evils. Thus their knowledge will be absolutely perfect, with respect to the removal of all delusion and deceit. The knowledge of the saints here is mixed with darkness, and in many things they are often deceived, have many errors and wrong thoughts, in one respect and another. But there is a perfect end of all such darkness in heaven. There is no such thing as blindness or deceit. There, light and darkness are no longer mixed together, as 'tis in the twilight; but there shall be only light without darkness, as 'tis in the perfect day, after the sun is risen.

Their holiness shall be absolutely perfect, with respect to the removal of all sin. There shall be no more corruption in the heart. There is no more actual sin.

The perfection of their happiness is absolute, as to what concerns the removal of all uneasiness or discontent. There is no more death, or sorrow or crying, but all tears are wiped away from their eyes. Rev. 7, at latter end, "And he that sitteth on the throne shall dwell among them. They shall hunger no more, neither thirst any more; neither shall the sun light on them, nor any heat. For the Lamb which is in the midst of the throne shall feed them, and shall lead them unto living fountains of waters: and God shall wipe away all tears from their eyes."[2]

The perfection of their peace is absolute with respect to the removal of all trouble of conscience, all disturbance by the temptations of Satan and the storms of an evil world. The perfection of their rest is absolute, as to the cessation of all toil and labor. Rev. 14:13, "Blessed are the dead which die in the Lord from henceforth: Yea, saith the Spirit, that they may rest from their labors; and their works do follow them."

I come now, to the

Second thing, which is to show how Christians are said to be come to the spirits of just men thus made perfect. And,

1. As we before observed of the angels,[3] so it may be said of "the spirits of just men made perfect," that they belong to the same society with them. And indeed they are of the same society, in a stricter sense than can be said of the angels: for the saints on earth are of the same company with the angels, as the company of the angels and the church of saints are two companies united together into one larger company consisting of these two parts, whereby the whole are said to be a company of two armies. But Christians on earth are not only come to "the spirits of just men made perfect" as they are of that same larger society, but they are also of the same particular company. They are of the same part of the two, which together constitute that larger company.

They are more properly said to be of the same church, and the same body of Christ, than the angels are: for they are in like manner united to Christ as mediator, as some of his redeemed church, his spouse that he has purchased by his blood, as the saints in heaven are; which can't be said of the angels.

2. Their own spirits are the spirits of just men, though not yet made perfect.

---

2. See MS sermon no. 565, on Rev. 7:17, Aug. 1740 (Beinecke Rare Book & Manuscript Library, Yale University).

3. See sermon no. 545, "the third place," on "The Innumerable Company of Angels," above (55–58).

3. They have the promise of the same state. They are entitled to it, and can't fail of it. So sure as Christ is in heaven, they themselves shall be there; yea, they shall be there very speedily. They are hastening thither, as on the wings of time. They have that faith and that hope, which, as an anchor of the soul, enters in there where they be, and there they themselves, all of them, will quickly be.

4. They have already the firstfruits of that glory in their souls. They have something of the same light, and the same beauty and the same joy. They have an earnest of their inheritance, which they enjoy. Those that [are] true Christians, eternal life is begun in them. It is, in a degree, abiding in them already; as is manifest by I John 3:15, "Whosoever hateth his brother is a murderer: and ye know that no murtherer hath eternal life abiding in him." Here the Apostle's argument supposes that others, that are true Christians and love the brethren, have eternal life abiding in them.

True Christians have that peace and joy in God, and in the Lord Jesus Christ, that is a foretaste of that blessedness which "the spirits of just men made perfect" enjoy.

5. They are coming nearer and nearer to the same perfection, with that which "the spirits of just men made perfect" are arrived at. For that grace that is implanted in them, which is the firstfruits of glory, is a growing thing. That light which they have, "shines more and more unto the perfect day," Prov. 4:18.

And that water that Christ has given them, is in them "as a well of water, springing up unto everlasting life," John 4:14. It springs up, and rises higher and higher, and grows greater and greater, like the waters of the sanctuary, till they shall become as the waters of a mighty river, Ezek. 47 at [the] beginning.

That seed that is sown in them, and abides in them, is a growing thing. It shoots forth roots deeper and deeper, and sprouts more and more, and is budding and blossoming; and the fruit, when ripe, will [be] the perfect glory of the saints in heaven.

APPLICATION.

Use I may be of *Instruction*.

First. This confutes the error of those that suppose that the soul sleeps till the resurrection. It has been already shown that the Apostle, in speaking of "the spirits of just men made perfect," must needs be understood [to speak] of the separate spirits of dead saints. Neither the words themselves, nor the context, will bear any other interpretation. And how does this consist with such a strange doctrine, which many have maintained, that the soul sleeps till the resurrection? If the soul of a good man after his death, is in a state of sleep and perfect insensibility, knowing and perceiving nothing any more than if it were in a state of annihilation, how absurdly would it be said to be made perfect! Is a state of perfect insensibility, and no way differing from nonexistence as to any perception or act, properly called a state of perfection?

And besides, if this were the state that the souls of dead saints were in, why should it be mentioned as such a great privilege, to be come to such spirits? What is there, in such a state of sleep and insensibility, that does in such a special manner show the great privilege, as having attained to the spirits of just men?

Second. What has been said, seems to afford great reason to suppose that the saints in heaven are acquainted with the state of the church on earth. For why should we suppose that God should so order it, that the saints in heaven, and the saints on earth, should be so nearly related one to another, as to be both the same society, the same family, the same spouse and body of Christ, and that they are all united in the same interest and the same inheritance, and shall soon all be together, and yet the saints in heaven be kept totally ignorant of the state of the church on earth?

Why should two parts of one society and family, be kept in ignorance one of another?

The saints in heaven, being so nearly related to the saints on earth, must needs be united to them in affection, and must be concerned for the flourishing and prosperity of the church on earth. And there is more reason in the nature of the thing, to suppose that they should rejoice at the conversion of a sinner on earth, than the angels: for they are more nearly related. But we are told

Sermon 6

expressly, that "There is joy in the presence of the angels of God over one sinner that repenteth," Luke 15:10.

That the saints in heaven are {acquainted with the state of the church on earth}, may be any otherwise argued. They are often represented in Revelation, as rejoicing and praising God for {his great and marvelous works, and his great judgments. That whole heavenly society is} called upon to rejoice: Rev. 18:20, "Rejoice over her, thou heaven."

And if we suppose that they are not acquainted, many absurdities must be maintained: [viz.,] the angels are certainly [not] acquainted [with what happens on earth]; the saints, that are every day going up to heaven, must forget {what has happened on earth}. And other arguments might be mentioned.

Use II may be of *Self-Examination*, whether you are come "to the spirits of just men made perfect"?

First. Are you just men? Are you so by the imputation of Christ's righteousness? Are you one that has no dependence on your own righteousness for justification, that have been made thoroughly sensible of your own unrighteousness, and you can't be justified or accepted on account of any righteousness of yours? And do you indeed trust in the righteousness of Christ, as having seen the excellency of the way of salvation by Christ? Do you rejoice in his righteousness, and in the thoughts of being saved by it, as being a way of being saved whereby you are abased, and Christ and free grace exalted?

And are you, in another sense, just men by inherent holiness? Are you one that is upright in heart? Do you delight in holiness, and hunger and thirst after it? And is indwelling sin your great burthen? Do you love God's law because of its holiness and strictness, and hate every evil and false way, and abhor yourself for your sins?

Are you one that is[4] righteous in your behavior towards God and towards men, one that "does justly, loves mercy and walks humbly with your God"?

4. MS: "are."

Is it your earnest endeavor, to keep "a conscience void of offense" [Acts 24:16]?

Second. Are you one that has[5] your delight in the saints? They that belong to that glorious society of saints, that are made perfect in holiness, they delight in the saints for their holiness. If they see any that they apprehend to be holy, their hearts are knit to them; they have complacence in the society of such. If you don't delight in the conversation of the holy, 'tis not likely that you belong to their society.

Third. Do you choose your inheritance in heaven, where those "spirits of just men made perfect" are? Is your heart weaned from the earth, by seeing things that appear to you sweeter and more excellent? And is your heart very much longing and thirsting after those glorious enjoyments, which "the spirits of just men made perfect" do enjoy there? Is this the inheritance you seek, and are daily laboring for?

Fourth. Have you the firstfruits of their glory in your soul? Have you had something of heaven's light shining into your heart, and do you feel heaven's love shed abroad there? Are you in some measure of an heavenly temper? Have you had some foretastes of their joy and peace? Does it seem to you that you know something [of] what Christ means, when he speaks of the water that he gives, being in a person as a spring "of water springing up into everlasting life" [John 4:14]?

Fifth. Do you make that perfection, which "the spirits of just men made perfect" have arrived to, your work? Are you not content with anything short of this? Don't it content you to think that you are already converted and sure of salvation? Don't you rest in past attainments? But is the breathing and struggle of your soul, to be more delivered from sin, this body of sin and death, this heavy clog of a sinful heart, that you [may] serve God more freely, and with more life and ardency of spirit, may live more to his glory? And are you thus as the Apostle was, who, "forgetting the things that were behind, pressed towards the mark for the prize of the high calling of God, which is in Christ Jesus" [Philip. 3:13–14]?

5. MS: "have."

Sermon 6

You should be strict in your examination of yourselves in these things, as it greatly concerns you to know what society you belong to, lest hereafter you be amazingly disappointed when your spirit comes to be separated from your body; and when you expected to go to the spirits of just men made perfect, you unexpectedly find yourself among the spirits in prison, the damned spirits of wicked men, that are perfect in wickedness and misery.

SERMON 7

How Christians Are Come to Jesus the Mediator of the New Covenant

Hebrews 12:22–24.

And to Jesus the mediator of the new covenant.

[I come now to the]
    VII. [Seventh] particular: [What these are come to, even the mediator of the new covenant]. In handling this point, I would [show],
    First. That a covenant between God and fallen creatures [requires a mediator].
    Second. What covenant that is that is spoken of in the text.
    Third. Why it is called a new covenant.
    Fourth. How Jesus Christ is the mediator of this new covenant.
    Fifth. How Christians are come to this mediator.

    And here, the
    First thing is, that a covenant between God and fallen creatures requires a mediator. It was not meet that God should have to do with fallen man in way of covenant, unless it was by a mediator. A covenant is a friendly transaction, or at least it is ever so in God towards his creatures. It is a manifestation of goodness and

wonderful condescension in God towards creatures, that he that is infinitely above 'em, should deal with them in such a way, and become obliged to creatures as one in covenant with them, who might deal with them only in a way of mere sovereignty. But it was not meet that an offended God should thus deal with a rebel, in such a way of condescension and friendliness, unless it was by a mediator, lest he should injure the honor of his majesty and justice.

Entering into covenant is always either the fruit of peace between the parties covenanting and agreeing, or it is in order to peace. But there can be no peace between God and rebels, but by a mediator. God and fallen men are enemies. God, as man's lawgiver and judge, most necessarily appears as the enemy of him who is under the guilt of sin; and the sinners, unless reconciled by a mediator, will remain an enemy of God.

The *Second* thing is, to inquire what covenant that is that is spoken of in the text.

Answer. 'Tis that covenant of grace that Christ promulgated when he came unto the world. 'Tis the covenant that God has revealed to the Christian church, or the covenant that God made with his people at Mt. Sion, wherein pardon and salvation are offered to sinners and promised to believers. The parties covenanting are God and believers. The benefits promised in this covenant are: peace with God, a reconciliation after God has been provoked and displeased, and his eternal wrath deserved; a deliverance from the guilt of sin, that God should no more look on those that are interested in the covenant as sinners, having no sin imputed to them; and that they should be delivered from the eternal damnation that is threatened by the law to all sinners, and from all other fruits of God's wrath and curse; and that they should have a real interest in the righteousness of Christ, and accepted therein as perfectly righteous in the eyes of God the Judge of all, and on the account of that righteousness, be received as the objects of the favor of God, and unto the state of the children of God. And that their natures should be more and more sanctified, that they should be delivered more and more from sin, and that they should have the image of God perfected in them. And that he would enable them to live holy lives and bring forth good fruit, and persevere in holiness to the end. And that he would, in a way of diligent and faithful serving him, give them the comforts of his spirit: peace of conscience and joy in the Holy Ghost, special manifestations of his glory and favor, and a joyful hope of eternal life. And that he would defend 'em from their enemies, that he would preserve 'em from Satan, and give 'em finally the victory over all enemies. And that at death their souls shall be perfectly freed from sin, shall ascend to be with Christ in paradise in a state of glory, their bodies being still united to Christ, resting in their graves till the resurrection; and that then they shall rise, the soul being united to the body again, which shall be made like to Christ's glorious body; and that they, in this risen state, shall be openly acquitted before the world of angels and men, receiving that blessed sentence, "Come ye blessed of my Father, inherit the kingdom prepared for you from the foundation of the world" [Matt. 25:34]; and that then they shall, both soul and body, enter into the kingdom that God has prepared {for them}, and shall enjoy eternal life in a state of perfect glory and blessedness forever and ever.

These are the benefits promised in the covenant. And the great condition of the covenant, is faith in Jesus, whereby the believer does with all his heart close with Christ as the Savior, renouncing all other saviors and lovers, and giving up themselves to him, to be united to him and to be his in all his offices.

This covenant is that which in Scripture is said to [be] a sure covenant, or a covenant "well-ordered in all things, and sure" [II Sam. 23:5], and an "everlasting covenant" [Gen. 17:7].

The *Third* thing is, to inquire why this covenant is called a new covenant. To such an inquiry, I

Answer, that 'tis called a new covenant with respect [to] that old covenant that was given forth from Mt. Sinai. "New" is a relative term, and has relation to something that, in comparison of it, is old. When the Scripture speaks of a new covenant, there is plainly supposed to have been some other covenant, in the room of which this succeeds. And still there is a reference in this to something that was of old, at Mt. Sinai: for in all the particulars mentioned in the three verses of the text, the comparison is carried on between the two mountains of Mt. Sinai and Mt. Sion. At Mt. Sion, the new covenant is given forth, as the old covenant was given forth from Mt. Sinai.

And there are two things that were exhibited at Mt. Sinai, with reference to which the covenant of grace, as revealed by Christ in the days of the gospel, is called a new covenant:

1. The covenant of works that God had formerly entered into with man in the state in which he was first created, was given forth at Mt. Sinai. The covenant of works was then given forth to the children of Israel. God did not properly then make a covenant of works with the children of Israel. He did not enter into a covenant of works with them, for they were not in a capacity for it; they were already fallen creatures, and so not capable of eternal life by such a covenant. But yet God did truly give forth the covenant of works from Mt. Sinai: he did at that time renewedly reveal and propose that covenant of works to the children of Israel from that mountain, for their conviction, to prove them and make them sensible of their own miserable and undone condition, and make 'em sensible of their necessity of a mediator. So the covenant of works was given out to 'em in all its strictness and severity, to be as a schoolmaster, and takes the church from its minority, and fits it for the coming of Christ. The law shut 'em up to the faith that should afterward be revealed.

'Tis certain that the covenant of works was then given forth to the children of Israel, because the Scripture, speaking of the covenant of grace and comparing law and gospel, and the works of the law with the faith of Jesus Christ, often speaks of the law as being given of old by Moses. Now the law thus spoken of, is the very same thing as the legal covenant, or, which is the same thing, the covenant of works. The law was given at Mt. Sinai with all its strictness and terrors, with its thunders and lightnings and curses, saying, "Cursed is every man that continues not [in all things which are written in the book of the law to do them]," Deut. 27:26, Gal. 3:10.

Now that is nothing else but giving forth the covenant of works with its strict exaction of perfect obedience, on pain of eternal damnation.

2. The covenant of grace, as given forth by Christ in the evangelical dispensation of it, is called a new covenant with the respect to the same covenant of grace in its old legal dispensation by Moses. Though the covenant of works was given forth at Mt. Sinai, yet that was not the only covenant that was revealed there to the children of Israel; if it had, it would have tended to drive them into despair. But there was a covenant that God did not only reveal, but which he properly entered into with that people at that mountain, whereby they became his covenant people, and were as it were espoused to himself.

And this could be no other than the covenant of grace. God did really reveal the covenant of grace at Mt. Sinai, though it was more obscurely by far than Christ afterward revealed it, and though it was delivered in more legal manner. God did really renew with the children of Israel in the wilderness that covenant that he had made with Abraham 430 years before, which the Scripture expressly teaches to be the covenant of grace. And therefore God, when he comes to that people in the wilderness, encourages 'em with that, that he was "the God of Abraham, of Isaac, and of Jacob."

The covenant of grace is virtually contained in those words in the preface to the Ten Commandments, which words God spoke at Mt. Sinai: "I am the Lord thy God which have brought thee out of the land of Egypt, out of the house of bondage" [Ex. 20:2]. It was only by the covenant of grace that God was the Lord their God, and the work of righteousness by Christ was represented by God's bringing them "out of the land of Egypt, out of the house of bondage," there spoken of. And the covenant of grace was obscurely contained in the ceremonial law that was given at Mt. Sinai, wherein such sacrifices were commanded, and so many things representing and shadowing forth the redemption of Christ.

Sermon 7

That old legal dispensation of the covenant of grace, though it was essentially the same covenant with that which Christ revealed in its evangelical dispensation, yet because it differed circumstantially, is sometimes spoken of in Scripture as another covenant. So it is in the 8th [chapter] of Hebrews, beginning with the 5th verse: "Who serve unto the example and shadow of heavenly things, as Moses was admonished of God when he was about to make the tabernacle: for, See, saith he, that thou make all things according to the pattern showed to thee in the mount." Here, the old covenant that he speaks of is manifestly the old, legal dispensation of Moses, and not the covenant of works, because he speaks of that covenant that the ancient priests were ministers of, and speaks of Christ as a mediator and minister of a better covenant than those priests were, as you may see.

And it appears more fully still in the beginning of the following chapter, the 9th chapter, v. 1: "Then verily the first covenant had also ordinances of divine service, and a worldly sanctuary."

The covenant that had these ordinances, was not the covenant of works, {but the covenant of grace}.

So that by new and old covenant in Scripture sometimes is meant the same as new and old testament: and therefore the phrases seemed to be used indifferently to signify the same thing. Where it is said in the text, that Christ was the mediator of the new covenant, in the margin it is "testament."[1] And we find both the phrases used in the same sense: in the 7th [chapter] of Hebrews, 22nd verse, 'tis said, Jesus was the "surety of a better testament"; in the next chapter, [ch.] 8, [v. 6,] 'tis said, "he is the mediator of a better covenant," both meaning the same thing.

The covenant of grace, as promulgated by Christ in its evangelical dispensation, seems to be called a new covenant with respect to those other constitutions, on two accounts:

(1) Because it succeeds them in order of time, and is established in their stead. First the covenant of works is revealed, and then the covenant of grace; and first the legal dispensation of the covenant of grace is established, and then the evangelical. The

---

1. I.e., in the margin of the King James Version.

latter dispensation takes [the] place of the former; the former waxing old and vanishing away, the latter is established in its stead. Heb. 8:13, "In that he saith, A new covenant, he hath made the first old. Now that which decayeth and becometh old is ready to vanish away."

(2) It seems also to be called a new covenant, on account of its superior excellency. Because artificial things are commonly in their best state while new, and because old things are removed to make way for new ones, for the sake of their superior excellency, therefore we find the word "new" sometimes denotes the great excellency of the thing that is said to be so. Thus Christ promises to him that overcomes, that he will give him a new name, Rev. 2:7; which imports that Christ will give him an excellent [name], and put upon him excellent honor and dignity. So the church is said to sing "a new song," Rev. 5:9; i.e., {an excellent song}.

And from time to time those spiritual things, that are spoken as new, are more excellent than the old. "[For behold, I create new] heavens and earth, and the old[2] shall not be remembered, nor come into mind" [Is. 65:17]. [The] New Jerusalem "cometh down out of heaven from my God: and I will write upon him my new name" [Rev. 3:12].

So the new covenant is a more excellent covenant than the old covenant of grace, {and} more excellent than [the] covenant of works, showing more of the glory of God. {It has} better promises, {and is} a surer covenant, {and is} an everlasting covenant. The first was sure on God's side, but uncertain on man's. But {the second is sure on both sides}.

So the evangelical dispensation is more excellent {than the old dispensation of grace. Under it, the} light [is] clearer {than under the old dispensation, and the} grace of God more manifest and more abundant {than under the old}. The most explicit promises, and those that are most insisted on, [are] more excellent {under the new covenant}.

---

2. KJV: "former."

Sermon 7

The church, with whom the covenant in its evangelical dispensation is made, [is] in a more spiritual, heavenly and excellent constitution.

I come now to the
Fourth thing proposed, which is to show how that Jesus Christ is the mediator of this new covenant.

As to the covenant of works, that had no mediator.

The covenant of grace in its old dispensation, which is sometimes called the old covenant, had a typical mediator, Moses.

Priests, high priests especially, as such entered into the Holy of Holies.

As has been observed before, the honor of God's majesty and justice will not suffer him to treat with a rebel by way of covenant, but by a mediator. And Christ is the mediator of the new covenant in the following respects:

1. He is the person who brings the covenant from God to us. Moses of old brought {the old covenant}. [He] received the word, [and brought it] to the people. "Speak thou with us," say they, Ex. 20:19.

[Moses] brought the tables of the covenant.

[He] wrote the book of the covenant.

And, as the priests, [he] instructed the people.

So [Christ] brought [the new covenant] down from heaven.

[Christ] reveals it, makes known the mind and will of God concerning men's salvation. Herein mostly consists his prophetical office. When he came, he brought it personally.

He sent his Spirit more fully to reveal it by his apostles, agreeable to his promise to them. "He shall take of mine, and shall show it unto you" [John 16:14].

He brings the covenant, and reveals it by his Spirit in effectual calling.

2. The promises of the covenant are first made to Christ, as the head and representative of all the elect, and through him are made to believers. Tit. 1:2, "In hope of eternal life, which God, that cannot lie, [promised before the world began]." II Tim. 1:9, "Who

hath saved us and called us." As of old, promises [were] made to Abraham as the father of [the children of Israel].

3. He is the mediator that has procured all the blessings promised in the covenant.

4. He is the person that has confirmed the blessings of the covenant, sealed with his blood.

5. The promises and blessings of the covenant are not obtained in any other way, but in union with him.

6. The consent to the covenant on our part, is brought to the Father through him. As Moses.

Our faith and prayers are of avail with God only through his hand.

7. He first receives the blessings of the covenant of grace of the Father, in himself as head.

8. He is the person through whom the blessings of the covenant are actually bestowed.

[The] *Fifth* inquiry is, how Christians are come to this mediator.

Answer. This implies three things:

1. They accept of him. Accepting of Christ by faith is very often called coming to him in Scripture. Christ invites heavy laden sinners to come to him, that he may give 'em rest [Matt. 11:28]; and promises that he that comes to him he "will in no wise cast out" [John 6:37].

2. They are united. Union with Christ is the first and most immediate consequence of an acceptance of him. Christians have vital union with Christ. They are come to him, and are ingrafted into him, become branches in him, members of his body. They are come to him, so that he is come to dwell with them and in them by his Holy Spirit. And there is also a relative union: they are come to be nearly related to Christ; their souls are brought to Christ, as the king's daughter is led in unto a glorious prince, to be united to him in spiritual wedlock. There is a covenant union between Christ and the soul of a Christian; they are united by the mutual bond

of a covenant, whereby he is theirs, and they, his. There is such an union, that they have a mutual propriety in each other.

There is a legal union between them, so that they are one in law, and looked upon and accepted as one in what concerns the law by God the Judge of all.

3. They are come to this mediator, as they [have] communion with him in his benefits. Communion is the immediate consequence of union, or a partaking of the benefits of Christ's mediation, such as freedom from guilt, peace with God, a joint participation of life and comfort, and a joint title to the eternal inheritance and kingdom.

And among other benefits, they are brought to [communion] of Christ's mediation. They have a title to dwell with Christ forever, to be where he is, and to behold his glory. John 17:24, "Father, I will that they also, whom thou hast given [me], should be [with me where I am]."

[APPLICATION.][3]

Use I may be to convince Christless sinners of their misery, in that they have no mediator to stand between God and them.

First. Consider, you are a stranger to the covenant of promise.

Second. The wrath of God [is] abiding upon [you].

Third. How dreadful it will be [to] die, and go and appear before God without a mediator.

Use II of *Exhortation*, to come to this mediator and trust in him.

First. Consider how fit a person Christ is for that office.

Second. [Consider] what he will do for you in it.

---

3. The following "Uses" appear on L. 8v. between points IV and V.

SERMON 8

How Christians Are Come to the Blood of Sprinkling

Hebrews 12:22–24.

And to the blood of sprinkling that speaks better things than the blood of Abel.

I come now, to the

[VIII.] Eighth, and last, particular spoken of in the text, and would now show how Christians are come "to the blood of sprinkling that speaks better things than the blood of Abel."

At first the Apostle tells the Christian Hebrews they were come to Mt. Sion, "the city of the living God," "the heavenly Jerusalem," and then proceeds to show what things they were come at or in Mt. Sion.

As has been before observed,[1] Mt. Sion being the mountain of the sanctuary, was the place where the sacrifices were slain and offered, and where the blood of the sacrifice was to be sprinkled on him for whom it was offered. The literal Mt. Sion of old was the place where the blood of the sacrifice was to be sprinkled upon

---

1. See the first in the sermon series, *Christians Are Come to Mt. Sion*, above (35–47).

Sermon 8

him that was to be cleansed from leprosy, agreeable to the direction in the 14th chapter of Leviticus.

When the old covenant, or the covenant of grace in its old dispensation, was made and confirmed with the children of Israel, Moses, who was the typical mediator of that old covenant, took the book of the covenant and read in the audience of the people; and when they had said, "All that the Lord hath said will we do, and be obedient, then Moses took the blood of the sacrifice, and sprinkled it on the people, and said, Behold the blood of the covenant, which the Lord hath made with you concerning all these words," of which we have an account in Ex. 24, 7th and 8th verses. This the Apostle takes notice of in this epistle to the Hebrews, as particularly, Heb. 9:18, etc., "Whereupon neither the first testament was dedicated without blood. For when Moses had spoken every precept to all the people according to the law, he took the blood of calves and of goats, with water, and scarlet wool, and hyssop, and sprinkled both the book, and all the people, saying, This is the blood of the testament which God hath enjoined unto you. Moreover he sprinkled with blood both the tabernacle, and all the vessels of the ministry. And almost all things are by the law purged with blood; and without shedding of blood is no remission."

That was the blood of sprinkling, by which the old covenant, or first testament, was confirmed. In the text, the Apostle speaks of the blood of sprinkling by which the new testament or covenant is confirmed.

Here I would [inquire]:

First. What blood this is.

Second. Why it is called the blood of sprinkling.

Third. What things the blood of Abel spake of old.

Fourth. How Christ's blood speaks better things than the blood of Abel.

Fifth. How Christians are come to this blood of sprinkling.

The *First Inquiry* is, What blood this is, that is here spoken of?

Answer. The blood of Christ. The blood of sprinkling, by which the covenant under the old dispensation was confirmed, was "the blood of goats and calves, with water, and scarlet wool and hyssop." But the blood by which the new covenant is confirmed, is Christ's own blood. As Heb. 9:23, "It was therefore necessary that the patterns of things in the heavens should be purified with these; but the heavenly things themselves with better sacrifices than these."

In the literal Mt. Sion, the blood of bulls and goats was the blood of sprinkling, by which the unclean was sanctified to the purifying of the flesh. But Christ's own blood is the blood that is sprinkled at the spiritual Mt. Sion, to purify the unclean soul. Heb. 9:11, etc., "But Christ being come an high priest of good things to come, by a greater and more perfect tabernacle, not made with hands, that is to say, not of this building; neither by the blood of goats and calves, but by his own blood he entered in once into the holy place, having obtained eternal redemption for us. For if the blood of bulls and of goats, and the ashes of an heifer sprinkling the unclean, sanctifieth to the purifying of the flesh: how much more shall the blood of Christ, who through the eternal Spirit offered himself without spot to God, purge your conscience from dead works to serve the living God?"

The *Second Inquiry* is, Why this blood of Christ is called the blood of sprinkling?

Answ. 1. Because it avails nothing but by being applied to the soul. However sufficient this blood is in itself, yet it can be of no service or benefit to us, unless 'tis applied to us. Our souls can't be cleansed by it, if no application be made of it.

This application is by means of two things: partly by a work of the Spirit working faith in that blood, awakening and convincing the soul, making it sensible of its need of the blood of Christ and making it sensible of the sufficiency of that blood, and bringing it to that "fountain that is set open for Judah and Jerusalem, for sin and for uncleanness" [Zech. 13:1]; and partly an act of grace, consequent of that work of the Spirit, justifying the sinner. By this, the guilt of sin is actually purged away, and the sinner, through the blood of Christ, stands perfectly clean or pure in the sight of God.

Sermon 8

Thus the blood of Christ is applied to the soul, and without such application, it can have no effect for its cleansing.

2. This application of the blood of Christ, was of old represented by sprinkling. So the blood of the sacrifices was to be sprinkled, and so the water of purifying, that represented the blood of Christ, was also to be sprinkled upon the persons that were to be cleansed by it, Num. 8:7. So the water of separation was to be sprinkled upon him that touched the dead body of a man, as in the 19th [chapter] of Numbers [Num. 19:11–13]; and hence 'tis prophesied of Christ in Is. 52:15, "that he should sprinkle many nations."

The *Third Inquiry* is, What things those were that were spoken by the blood [of] Abel, that are referred to in the words?

Answ[er]. The blood of Abel cried for vengeance. Abel, if he was not the first good man that died, yet he was in all probability the first good man that was put to death for his righteousness. For Abel was so, and was slain for his righteousness. I John 3:12, "Not as Cain, who was of that wicked one, and slew his brother. And wherefore slew he him? Because his own works were evil, and his brother's righteous."

He was one of Christ's. He was a member of the mystical body, or of the church of Christ, and seems in his day to have been the chief of the holy seed that God had in the world; and therefore the cruelty that was done to him, was in some sense done to Christ. As Christ says, "In that ye have done it to one of the least of these my brethren, ye have done it unto me" [Matt. 25:40].

He may be looked upon as the first that ever died a martyr, that was persecuted to death for his piety.

His blood cried from the ground to God; as God says to Cain, Gen. 4:10, "The voice of thy brother's blood crieth to me from the ground." Thus the blood had a voice. It spoke after he was dead, which is what the Apostle has reference to in Heb. 11:4, "By faith Abel offered unto God a more excellent sacrifice than Cain, by which he obtained witness that he was righteous, God testifying of his gifts: and by it he being dead yet speaketh." His blood spoke as it cried to God, and what it cried to him for was his wrath and curse on him that had made himself guilty of his blood.

[The] *Fourth Inquiry* is, How the blood of Christ speaks better things than the blood of Abel? The blood of these two persons might well be compared thus together, because they were both righteous, though one but imperfectly and the other perfectly; so the one by a derivative, dependent righteousness, the other had righteousness in himself. And they both were hated, and their blood shed for their righteousness, and both died by the malignity of the sin and corruption of mankind. It was the sin of man that killed Abel, and so it was the sin of man that killed Christ. The nature and tendency of sin is to attempt to kill God, as appeared by what came to pass in fact when God became man, and was capable of being killed. And the same sinners that are saved by the blood of [Christ], have in effect been guilty of killing of Christ: for that sin that they had in their hearts was of this nature, and the sins that they committed showed, if it had been in their power, they would do it. And the consequence of their sins, has actually been the death of Christ. Their sins were costly to Christ: they cost him his blood. But yet his blood don't cry for vengeance to those sinners that come to him, as Abel's did.

1. But Christ's blood cries for peace and pardon for the guilty, for those that have been his murtherous enemies when they come to him. This is the voice of his blood to God: "Let these poor, sinful, wretched [sinners] who have hated me, and have been my malicious, murtherous enemies, let them be forgiven; let all their iniquities be blotted out; let not that wrath be executed upon them that they deserve, but let 'em have peace with thee. Let 'em not have terror of conscience, as Cain had, but let 'em be delivered from the spirit of bondage. And let 'em have peace of conscience, the peace of God that passes all understanding."

2. It cries to God that they may be received to the state, and favor and inheritance of children. Abel's blood cried to God that Cain might be looked upon or treated as an enemy, that he might be banished from God and thrust out of his house, as it were to

Sermon 8

be a fugitive and vagabond in the [earth], that he might be driven from God's face and afar off. He went "and dwelt in the land of Nod," i.e., "in the land of banishment" [Gen. 4:16].

But Christ's blood, on the contrary, cries to God that sinners, his murtherers that are far off, might be brought nigh; that they mayn't be kept out of his house, but on the contrary be brought into his house, and be of the household of God, and might be received as children into the favor of God. Eph. 2:13–14, "But now in Christ Jesus ye who sometimes were far off are made nigh by the blood of Christ. For he is our peace, who hath made both one, and hath broken down the middle wall of partition between us"; [v.] 19, "Now therefore ye are no more strangers and foreigners, but fellow citizens with the saints, and of the household of God." His blood cries to God that they[2] may be entitled to a glorious inheritance; not that they might be slain in revenge, as Abel's blood cried for the death of Cain, but that they may have eternal life.

There are three things in the blood of Christ, by which it speaks such things: its appointment of God the Father for that end, and Christ's design in offering it up to God, and its sufficiency to merit them.

(1) Christ was appointed of God to be an high priest, to offer up his blood to these ends, that he might secure such things as these for sinners.

(2) It was Christ's design in shedding his blood thereby, to obtain these good things for sinners that should come to him. This was not only the will of the Father, but it was Christ's will. It was a thing agreed upon between the Father and the Son, that his blood should be spilt for this end. And when the Father sent him into the world on this errand, he most willingly came; he said, "Lo I come: I delight to do thy will, O my God: yea, thy law is within my heart" [Ps. 40:7–8]. To save poor sinners, his murtherous enemies, was the thing that moved him to yield himself up to be slain. He loved us, and gave himself for us [Eph. 5:2, Gal. 2:20]. He had a great and earnest desire that sinners might obtain these good things, and to that end he spilt his blood. His laying down his life was but an

2. MS: "he."

expression of this desire: for this he earnestly prayed a little before his blood was shed, for this he offered up strong crying and tears, even while his blood was issuing forth in that bloody sweat that he was the subject of in the garden. It was for these good things that he wrestled with God so earnestly in the days of his flesh, when he was in such an agony,[3] "and his sweat was as it were great drops of blood, falling down to the ground" [Luke 22:44]. Heb. 5:7, "Who in the days of his flesh, when he had offered up prayers and supplications with strong crying and tears unto him that was able to save him from death, and was heard in that he feared."

(3) The blood of Christ is sufficient to merit these good things. As this was the design of offering of it up, so it was precious enough to answer this design.

[The] *Fifth Inquiry* [is], How Christians are come to this blood? They are so, in three respects:

1. Their hearts close with the way of salvation by this blood. They don't seek salvation by any atonement and righteousness of their own. They are not vainly conceited of their own reformations, and tears, and prayers and other religious performances, to procure these good things for them. They despair in all that is their own, and see the insufficiency of that; but they are sensible of the preciousness and sufficiency of Christ's blood, and they are made sensible of the excellency of the way of salvation by it, and savor that way and delight in it. So they do in their hearts come to the fountain of his blood, come to that sacrifice, that they may be sprinkled with the blood.

2. They have received an interest in that blood in their hearty acceptance: Christ's atonement became theirs. The satisfaction that he has made to divine justice by his blood is imputed to them, and is looked upon [as] theirs, much as if they themselves had paid the debt.

3. Some of the good things that that blood cries to God, are already bestowed upon them, and a title to the rest. They have

---

3. See sermon on Luke 22:44 (no. 521), Oct. 1739, on Christ's agony (WJEO Vol. 54).

already the forgiveness of sins and peace with God. They have received the atonement, and are reconciled. They are already received as the sons of God, being made nigh by the blood of Christ. They have already received peace of conscience; they have already received the earnest of their future inheritance. And that eternal glory that is purchased by Christ's shedding his blood, as an act of obedience to the Father, is what they have a title to, and shall soon be possessed of.[4]

[APPLICATION.]

[The] Application is only in an *Use* of *Exhortation,* to exhort poor, guilty, condemned sinners, to come to the fountain of Christ's blood, that their hearts may be sprinkled from an evil conscience.[5]

First. Consider that if you finally continue to neglect and reject Jesus Christ, his blood will speak worse things against you, than the blood of Abel did against Cain. If you will accept Christ, and hearken to his gracious calls and invitations, it will cry to God for pardon {and peace for the guilty}. But if you despise Christ and tread his blood underfoot, it will cry to God for a more terrible vengeance than ever Cain suffered, in that he never enjoyed the light that you enjoy, nor ever had such glorious offers of mercy as you have had. You, having made a profession of the name of Christ, will be looked upon as a betrayer and murtherer of him, as Judas was, who murtherously betrayed his professed Lord and Master with a kiss; who, Christ tells us, had greater sin than Pilate that condemned him to die. John 19:11, "He that delivered me to thee hath the greater sin."

Judas was guilty of the blood of Christ in a higher degree than Pilate, and that blood of Christ cried for a very dreadful wrath against him; and it will cry for a like dreadful, amazing vengeance against you, if you who profess yourself to be a Christian don't

---

4. The remainder of L. 6v, and the entirety of L. 7r., are blank.

5. Here, a paragraph appears by itself at the bottom of L. 7v., and which Edwards encircled with a solid line, suggesting that he intended to relocate it; thus it has been moved to the end of the Application.

heartily seek after Christ and receive him, but continue to reject and despise. Well would it have been for you, if Christ had never come into the world and spilt his blood. Instead of being saved by it, it will be an occasion of your much more dreadful misery. You will only sink so much the deeper into hell. As it is said that Christ, who is "a sure foundation" {to those that believe, so to those who reject him he} will be "a stone of stumbling and rock of offense," Is. 8:14.

Though the blood of Christ speaks so much better things than the blood of Abel, and cries to God for such exceeding favor, and such excellent privileges and eternal glory for those that come to Christ, yet no blood cries for such vengeance as the blood of Christ, if it be trampled on and despised.

Second. Consider the great encouragements there are for you to come to this blood for cleansing. I shall mention but two at this time:

(1) Christ has not only shed this blood, but he has entered into glory with [it, along with his wounds, Rev. 5:6].

(2) 'Tis through this blood that multitudes of poor, guilty wretches have been cleansed and saved, from the beginning of the world hitherto.[6]

Those things show the abundant fullness of this fountain and [its] sufficiency to cleanse from all sin. Let them therefore encourage you to come also, that you may have a part with those multitude of happy souls that from the beginning of the world have been washed in that blood [Rev. 1:5; 7:14].

---

6. The concluding paragraph has been moved from the beginning of the Application.

Index

Abel, 33–35, 116–17, 119–21, 123–24
affections, 7, 53
angels, 19, 21, 23–25, 29, 31, 35, 37, 43, 54–64, 66–67, 72, 74–77, 86, 94, 100, 102–3, 108
Application, 9, 12
archangel, 24
ark, 23, 38–39, 43, 49–50
Arminian, 5
assembly, 25–26, 29, 35, 37, 67–70, 75, 77–79, 94
awakenings, 15

"Blank Bible," 18
blood, 28, 33–35, 88, 100, 114, 116–24
blood of Christ, 117–24
blood of sprinkling, 33–34, 116–19
Bull, Nehemiah, 17

Cain, 119–21, 123
Charity and Its Fruits, 15, 19
communion, 22, 33, 115
Connecticut Valley Awakening, 15, 16
conscience, 80, 96, 100, 104, 108, 118, 120, 123

conversion, 18, 20, 25, 34, 66, 102
conviction, 23, 30, 53, 90, 92, 109
covenant of grace, 18, 29, 32, 87–89, 107, 109–14, 117
covenant of redemption, 28
covenant of works, 32, 109–13

day of judgment, 18–20, 25, 55, 61, 63, 78, 98
death, 19, 25, 27, 59–61, 97, 99, 102, 104, 108, 119–22
departed saints, 31, 68, 94, 96–98
Directions, 13, 45–46
discourses, 3, 14, 15
Discourse on the Trinity, 29
Discourses on Various Important Subjects, 4, 14, 16
Divine and Supernatural Light, 9, 16
Doctrine, 9–12
Doddridge, Philip, 18, 21
duty, 7, 60

East Windsor, 5
Edwards, Sarah Pierpont, 17
Edwards, Susannah, 17
Edwards, Timothy, 5, 6
economy, 28, 83

Index

elect, 18, 19, 25–26, 61, 75, 76, 113
England, 16, 17
epidemic, 17
Esau, 27
excellency, 4, 6, 98–99, 103, 112, 122
experience, 10–12

faith, 27, 32, 74, 88, 101, 108–9, 114, 118
Faithful Narrative, 16
Family Expositor, 18
firstborn, 25–26, 35, 37, 68–79, 94

general assembly, 21, 25, 29, 35, 37, 68–70, 75, 78, 94
Global Sermon Editing Project, xi
glory, 5,
God the Judge, 18, 27–29, 37, 81–82, 87, 89, 91, 94, 107, 115
gospel, 5
grace, 87–90
Great Awakening, xi, 7, 15

Hadley, 17
Hampshire Association, 17
happiness, 30, 44, 63, 90–91, 99
Harris, Howell, 17
heart, 5, 7
heaven, 6
heavenly Jerusalem, 21–23, 35–37, 48, 50–51, 53, 94
hell, 7, 19, 31, 62, 78, 124
History of the Work of Redemption, 20
Hopkins, Samuel, 17

Improvement, 12, 13

innumerable company, 23–25, 29, 35, 37, 52, 54, 59, 75, 94, 100
invisible church, 68

Jebus, 50
Jebusites, 37, 38,
Jerusalem, 23
Judas, 123
just men, 18, 30, 32, 35, 37, 93–96, 100–105
justification, 32

knowledge, 8, 99

Manuductio, 5
Marsden, George, 17, 22
Massachusetts, 3
Mather, Cotton, 5
means of grace,
measles, 17
Mediator, 28–30, 32–33, 35, 37, 55, 82–86, 92, 94, 100, 106–7, 109, 111, 113–15, 117
meetinghouse, 16
Melchizedek, 49–50
method, 21, 37
Michael, 24, 58
Millo, 38
ministers, 2, 3, 5, 6
Miscellanies, 1, 2, 19
Moses, 21
Mt. Hermon, xii
Mt. Moriah, 39, 43
Mt. Sion, xii, 20–23, 28–29, 33, 35–37, 39–46, 87–90, 92, 94, 107, 109, 116, 118

new covenant, 32–33, 82, 88, 94, 106, 108–13, 118
New England, xi
New York City, 16
Northampton, 3, 15, 16

Index

nothingness, 31

Observation, 11
Owen, John, 18

perfection, 31
perfections, 23
Peter, 61, 94
preaching, 1–12,
principle,
privileges, 21–22, 26–27, 29, 44, 72, 74–77, 79, 87–88, 124
Propositions, 11, 12
providence, 23–24, 28, 52, 55, 83, 97
Puritan, 3–4, 18

religion, 5, 7, 8
Religious Affections, 7
revival, 7
rock, 37, 41–42, 46, 124

sacrament day, 22, 45n
sacrifices, 33, 46, 71, 73–74, 110, 116, 118–19
Satan, 24, 26, 63, 66, 78, 100, 108
satisfaction, 34
satisfaction (legal), 29, 34, 82–84, 122
Sinners in the Hands of an Angry God, 16

sleeping rocks, 31
Solomon, 39, 60
Some Thoughts, 7
soul sleep, 19, 31, 102
Stockbridge, 10,
Stoddard, Solomon 3, 5, 6

Text, 9, 10
time, 26, 32,
Trinity, 28–29, 82–85
True and False Christians, 15
True Excellency of a Minister of the Gospel, 6

understanding, 6, 21, 87, 98, 120
union, 24, 33, 56–57, 75, 89, 92, 114–15
use, 12
Uses, 13

visible church, 22

Wales, 17
water, 31, 60, 100, 101, 104, 117–19
Watts, Isaac, 19
worship, 26

Wesleys, 17
West Springfield, 17
Westfield, 17
Whitefield, George, 16, 17

www.ingramcontent.com/pod-product-compliance
Lightning Source LLC
Chambersburg PA
CBHW020854160426
43192CB00007B/924